The Beginner's Book of Chant

*A Simple Guide for Parishes
Schools and Communities*

by

A Benedictine Monk

SAINT MICHAEL'S ABBEY PRESS

MMIII

Saint Michael's Abbey Press
Saint Michael's Abbey
Farnborough
Hampshire. GU14 7NQ

Telephone +44 (0) 1252 546 105
Facsimile +44 (0) 1252 372 822
www.farnboroughabbey.org
info@farnboroughabbey.org

www.theabbeyshop.com

First edition: St Michael's Abbey Press 2003
Second edition: 2015 & 2022

Nihil obstat: Monsignor Jeremy Garratt, V.G.
Imprimatur: Right Reverend Crispian Hollis
Portsmouth, 3rd March 2003

The *Nihil obstat* and *Imprimatur* are a declaration that a book or pamphlet is considered to be free from doctrinal or moral error. It is not implied that those who have granted the *Nihil obstat* and *Imprimatur* agree with the contents, opinions or statements expressed.

ISBN 978 0 907077 39 8

Design and typesetting by Peter Harden

The fonts for the chant and modern music examples were devised at St Meinrad Archabbey and are available as Meinrada, Meinradb and Meinradc (four-line) and Melody A, Melody B and Melody C (five-line). Chant excerpts are © Abbaye S. Pierre de Solesmes and are reproduced with permission.

A catalogue record for this book is available from the British Library.

CONTENTS

Foreword   v

I   Historical Overview   1
II   Notation   7
III   Tutorial 1: Mass XVIII   15
IV   Rehearsal methods   23
V   Latin pronunciation   37
VI   Tutorial 2: Gloria XV   45
VII   Genre: *antiphons, psalms, hymns, other forms.*   53
VIII   Accompaniment   59
IX   Vernacular adaptations   63
X   Frequently asked questions   69

Appendices
1 The modes   77
2 Table of transcribed neumes   78
3 The Rhythmic controversy   80
4 Glossary   81

Further Reading   88

FOREWORD

Why yet another book on Gregorian Chant? Many books have talked about chant as if it were a dead science. It is a living art form. Indeed, one that has experienced a revival in recent years.

This guide is offered to those beginners who wish to dive head-first into the singing of the chant. Examples taken are those which are likely to be first encountered; most are found in an inexpensive volume of selected chants published by the monks of Solesmes, the *Liber Cantualis.*

The method offered for singing the chant is essentially practical. It does not claim to be 'authentic' but it is simple to understand and teach, and can be easily used and adapted by musicians working in the parish.

A lot of questions about the singing of chant can be answered by looking at its history. One article, in a noted magazine, stated that we can say virtually nothing about Gregorian chant before the 9th century. Catholic tradition maintains a degree of Divine intervention: the picture of a bird whispering in the ear of Pope St Gregory the Great (c.540-604) - which may be closer to the truth than many sceptics would allow. The origins are admittedly mysterious. A few clues however give us a glimpse of from where the chant may have come:

(i)   There are striking similarities between some of the psalm tones (for example *Tonus Peregrinus*) and melodic material found in ancient sources, particularly traditional Jewish music.

(ii) The system of eight modes traditionally applied to link Gregorian chant with Classical Antiquity does not always fit the music.

(iii) Chant is very natural to the human voice (this seems to transcend the East-West division in Christianity). Its intervals and patterns are easy to imitate - after a few tries - and the larger part of the repertoire is made up from stock phrases or 'units' rearranged in different patterns. It seems likely that the origins of chant are closely associated with improvised music.

The chant that was noted down in Pope St Gregory's day can be likened to pebbles in a stream. Different coloured pebbles have come from different lines of stone further up the hill and as they are washed downstream they are smoothed and take on a fairly similar appearance. The water rushing over them further smoothes them and they begin to appear to lock into each other. Similarly because not one system can explain the origins of the chant it is thankfully exonerated from accusations of being an invented music system. Like all 'natural' music it has a history of evolution and organic development - indeed with new vernacular adaptations and compositions based on chant styles it may be thought to be still evolving.

Sacred Scripture gives us some hint at the diversity of early Christian song. As part of the sacrifice of common worship, the early Christians brought with them psalms, hymns and spiritual songs to perform at the early worship services. Given the diversity of backgrounds within the Corinthian Church one may presume a wide variety of music styles were present at these services - perhaps memories of how the psalms used to be sung in the Temple or the way choruses were sung in classical plays, a snatch of a tune thought up at work, a folk song remembered from childhood. To this extraordinary melting pot probably needs to be added an element of ecstatic song made up on the spot. Of this we know very little and we only get glimpses of it in the long *jubilus* found at the end of many Alleluia verses;

[see Alleluia 'Specie tua', *GR* p. 416]

The stepwise and upward movement of these phrases, together with some of the most common intervals, suggest that these are stylised forms of music, expressions of joy originally improvised but gradually repeated until they were committed to memory and then ultimately written down. There is a remarkable coincidence with Christian communities practising ecstatic song today ('singing in the spirit') where much of this music reflects the cadences and shape of chant, indeed also its modality can be heard. This is of course not conclusive proof for the origins of chant but rather another part of the jigsaw.

Collection and codification

From around the beginning of the 8th century, in response to the need for local communities to have books to match the 'mother' church, the decline of improvisatory skills and the need for liturgical resources for church musicians, the collection and codification of Church chant commenced. Whilst the origin of the chants in Pope St Gregory's collection may have been largely within his Roman circle we may presume that some gathering from further afield went on with material being gained from visiting cantors. Whilst the collecting of liturgical texts and their origins can be traced, the transmission of the music that went with these texts is a bit of a mystery. We know that the famous cantors of Rome were dispatched to teach their art at the ends of the Empire and that presumably they picked up material during their visits and brought it back to Rome. Memory work seems to have been essential and, whilst this seems a gargantuan task, if one remembers that sixty-four of the *Alleluias* in common use today can be traced to one of eight basic melodies, which were then elaborated to fit the texts, the hypothesis seems more plausible.

Whilst this first codification of the chant seems a harmless enough exercise, and really a by-product of missionary efforts, it did have the unfortunate effect of causing older versions of chants, and even some whole families of chants, to disappear before they had been written down. If we knew more about these chants we could probably make better connections with the music of the ancient world.

With the development of a common group of chants, used widely, and the general expansion of resources, musically and liturgically, came the growth in theorising about the nature of the chant itself. This culminated in two ways. First, in the appearance of a variety of notations for the chant, and secondly, in a proliferation of writings on the chant. These theories arguably placed a straight jacket on the nature of the chant itself forcing conformity to the favoured eight mode system borrowed from Classical music theory. With this development the oral tradition of teaching chant starts to fade.

Rise of polyphony

During the 12th to 16th centuries the original monodic chant became obscured in the rise of polyphony. It became subservient to the new multi-voiced compositions which, whilst using the chant in their underlying structure, removed any clear indication of the rhythmic properties of the chant. The conventions of modality were retained by the rhythmic complexity caused by the additional voices and led to a separation between mode and rhythm. The new rules designed to guide the composition of polyphony became applied to the old chant melodies themselves. By the time of the Council of Trent, when Humanist interests nearly suppressed polyphony all together, the melodic form of the chant had been altered considerably. In the wake of this Council the Medicæan Gradual, possibly edited with the connivance of Palestrina and Anerio, enshrined forms of the chant melodies which had been finally altered to fit contemporary views on word stress. Multiple notes on single syllables were reduced and modally ambiguous pieces were altered to fit the eight mode model - all in the name of 'ancient practice'.

Restoration

This essentially remained the position for the next 300 years. The main publications of chant up until 1870 transmitted these forms of the melodies from the Medicæan editions. With the re-founding of Solesmes, in the mid-19th century, the modern study of chant commenced through a sincere attempt to restore the ancient form of the melodies. By collecting and collating chant manuscripts the monks developed a plausible method of decoding the neumatic symbols of the earliest extant manuscripts. This culminated in the publication of a series of facsimiles and 'performing' editions of the rediscovered chant melodies. A significant part of the Solesmes editorial work was the addition of rhythmic signs to the melodies indicating the presence or likelihood of rhythmic variation in what otherwise appeared to be a succession of equal length notes. Similar restoration work was undertaken in Germany with surprisingly different results. However, the Solesmes method (as it came to be known), retained dominance through official approval at the highest levels and because of the relatively simple means it gave to interpret the chant. These means were popularised through repeated editions of the *Liber Usualis* and through a wealth of text books aimed at Catholic school children and congregations.

In America Mrs Justine Ward's *Gregorian Chant* provided a detailed exposition of the Solesmes method for Catholic high schools. In Britain the publication, in two volumes, of *Plainsong for Schools*, with an important preface by the nuns of Stanbrook, popularised the chant. For choirmasters the Solesmes method was popularised through 'primers' by Dom Aldhelm Dean and Dom Alphege Shebbeare. Recordings further disseminated the Solesmes style of performance.

We should not presume that the Solesmes method was left unchallenged. Significant voices were raised against the 'equal notes' approach both on the Continent and in Britain. Dom Gregory Murray published a series of articles proposing a radically different interpretation of the early manuscripts and within the Solesmes family itself there were voices questioning the simplicity of the Gajard approach, leading to some controversy and bitterness on the eve of the Second Vatican Council. This rhythmic controversy is briefly summarised in Appendix 3.

Current situation

The Second Vatican Council (1962-1964) called for a reform of the chant books in two directions. The first was the production of a collection of simpler chants adapted for the use of smaller resources and conforming to the revised calendar and lectionary. This was completed with the release of the *Graduale Simplex* (1967) containing the *Kyriale Simplex* which had been circulated a few years earlier. In 1975 the revised *Graduale Romanum* appeared, the work of Solesmes who then commenced a series of editions for monastic use and two volumes for popular use, the *Liber Cantualis* and the *Gregorian Missal*. The first steps towards a critical edition of the *Graduale Romanum* were completed in 1990 with the publication of the *Graduale Triplex* which superimposed neumes from the most important early sources on the standard text.

The position of the chant since the wider introduction of vernacular liturgy has been ambiguous. Whilst Latin, and its chant, remained normative for the Western Church in practice, its use in the 20 years following the Second Vatican Council became limited to monasteries, some cathedrals, a handful of parishes and numerous special interest groups. Chant retained a small dedicated following in the academic world keen to study it as a means of understanding the development of Western music. An occasional release from a major record company provided some interest, and some scholars turned their attention to alternative repertoires of chant: the variants found in Sarum, Ambrosian, Beneventan and Mozarabic sources.

The current explosion of interest in the chant was heralded in the late 1980s by the inclusion in several pop songs of material sampled from Chant recordings. This did little to prepare us for the reception that greeted the recording *Canto Gregoriano* from the monks of Santo Domingo de Silos. The reasons for this renewed interest are partly due to commercial genius but also to the spiritual interest which seems to affect world cultures at the moment.

chapter two

NOTATION

Gregorian chant is most often associated with the peculiar notation that it uses. Whilst there is nothing particularly ancient about this style - it belongs to this side of the second millennium - it provides certain problems for those who are used to modern five-line notation where both rhythm and pitch are absolute. This is the beauty of the four-line notation. What its symbols give is an indication of their relationship relative to one another rather than to some external standard. As such it is free to be adapted to local situations and most importantly to the meaning of the text.

Pitch

Gregorian notation is written on a set of four lines (a stave or staff).

Unlike modern five-line notation this four-line notation does not indicate a definite pitch but rather the relationship of pitch between the notes. The key to this is the clef at the beginning of a composition. There are two different clefs (these can move up and down the stave). Their position defines where the semitone (*US Eng:* halfstep) falls.

Do clef   *Fa* clef

The important thing to remember is that the interval between a note on the line that is bracketed by the clef and a note in the space beneath this, is always a semitone:

semitone   *semitone*

Thus a scale written with a *do* clef would have the following disposition of tones (T) and semitones (S).

A scale written with a *fa* clef would have the following disposition of tones and semitones:

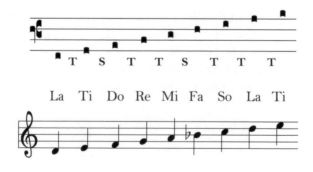

Duration

The basic Gregorian note is called the *punctum.*

This unit is the building block from which all combinations of notes in the four-line system are made. Its exact pitch and duration are chosen by the leader of the singing. Once it is given these values, at the beginning of the piece, they remain the same. Its duration, if you are counting, is a single count of '1', unless one of two modifications are made.

The first of these is indicated by a dot, like a full stop (*US Eng:* period), which makes the note twice its original length, or if found at the end of a piece, three times its length, or possibly even more.

Secondly, in modern editions, since the beginning of the twentieth century, a horizontal line can appear over the note. There is a remarkable range of possibilities on how to interpret this *horizontal episema.* We will treat it as having the same effect as the dot.

There are other variations on the basic *punctum* note form, however in simple use they are all treated as equal. A fuller listing is given in Appendix 2 but be aware of them from the beginning:

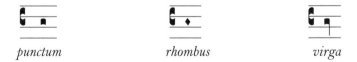

punctum   *rhombus*   *virga*

You will find very few pieces in the standard books which consist of just single notes. More often, multiple notes are assigned to one syllable. In these single syllable units one rule needs to be kept in mind. When you have one note on top of another the lower note is sung first. Thus:

 is interpreted

Next we meet the *vertical episema* (not to be confused with the *horizontal episema*, see above):

The *vertical episema* can have a lengthening effect on a note in the following four situations (in each case the note holding the episema directly above or below is the note to be lengthened):

One final form of note should be observed. This is the *quilisma*, which always appears as part of a group, and has the effect of doubling the length of the note immediately preceding it. It looks like a jagged rising figure:

Other important markings

(a) The flat sign

The pitch of a note may be lowered by a semitone (*US Eng*: half-step) by the placing of a flat sign before the note:

This correction lasts for the length of the word or occasionally for the phrase. Very rarely the modern natural sign will be used in complex phrases to bring the pitch back to normal.

(b) Barlines

These should not be interpreted like modern barlines but rather should be taken as recommendations from the editors as to where logical breaks should be made.

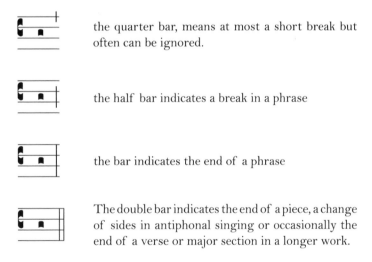

the quarter bar, means at most a short break but often can be ignored.

the half bar indicates a break in a phrase

the bar indicates the end of a phrase

The double bar indicates the end of a piece, a change of sides in antiphonal singing or occasionally the end of a verse or major section in a longer work.

Other performing directions

A few other symbols are essential in starting to sing the chant. The appearance of an asterisk (*) indicates a change in the number of singers. At the beginning of a composition you will find a phrase that looks like this:

[Sanctus: Mass XVIII *GR* pp. 767-768]

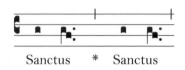

Sanctus   *   Sanctus

The asterisk here indicates that the first *Sanctus* is sung by a solo voice (or a smaller group of voices) and that the second *Sanctus* and what follows is sung by the full chorus. A similar division of duties is indicated by the use of the symbol ℣. which indicates a passage to be sung by smaller forces, a solo voice or group of voices. If you are singing with a small group of four then it would be logical to use one voice. If you are singing with a larger group, and especially in a larger building, then a small group would be appropriate. Occasionally you may find asterisks at the end of compositions, particularly the end of the Alleluia verses. This is the point where the whole choir would have come in, quietly, before the return of the Alleluia itself. In practice this takes some effort to achieve musically and should probably be put off until some experience has been gained in chant singing.

At the end of a section of text you may find the Latin word *bis*. This simply means to sing the section twice. In older publications you may find Latin numeration *ij* for twice and sometimes *iij* for three times.

The opening of a chant gives a wealth of information. Taking the first *Kyrie* of Mass XVIII as an example we find the following:

[*Kyrie*: Mass XVIII *GR* p. 767]

XI. s.

Y- ri- e * e- le- i -son. *bis* Christe e- le- i- son. *bis*

Working again from left to right, the initial letter of the composition is enlarged and placed before the clef. This draws the eye immediately to the beginning of the composition. Above this letter is the Roman numeral for four (**IV**). This indicates in which mode the chant is written. At the right hand side, above the stave is another Roman numeral in this case XI indicating that the earliest known manuscript for this chant comes from the 11th century ('s' for *siècle*). At the end of the music we find a small note drawn with a tail. This, called the custos, indicates what the first pitch of the next line of music will be.

To transcribe or not to transcribe?

The temptation for anybody attempting to introduce chant to a group new to the notation is to transcribe compositions out in to the familiar five-line notation of modern music. Modern notation editions of the *Liber Usualis* do exist, although they are fairly hard to find, and the six months or so that it takes to make the transition to four-line is well worth the freedom it offers. Those who have perfect pitch will not be bothered by hearing particular pitches when you are transposing a chant (and believe me you will!) and those with a little knowledge of the stress and rhythm implications of notation with barlines and time signatures will not be tempted to put stress where it is not wanted. Finally, whilst modern transcriptions can offer some excellent interpretational ideas to choirmasters new to chant they do tend to over-edit, adding nuances that do not belong to the music itself but stand rather as an opinion of how the music should be sung.

chapter three

TUTORIAL I: MASS XVIII

In the previous chapter we were introduced to the basics of notation. This tutorial aims to be a systematic working through of Mass XVIII as found in the 1975 *Graduale Romanum* (pp.767-768). It is relatively simple and is a Mass setting that could be put into use very swiftly. A sense of achieving something quickly is important with choirs of all sorts and this particular Mass setting has found considerable popularity with groups new to the chant.

Mass XVIII is recommended for *ferias* in Advent and Lent and for Masses for the Dead. This is a recommendation and should not be taken as a rule. It is perfectly suitable for use on any day of the year. The only thing that it is missing is the *Gloria*. You may find it useful to use a *Gloria* from another collection (say Mass VIII or Mass XV) when needed. The second *Kyrie* setting from Mass XVIII (marked 'B') traditionally belongs to the Mass for the Dead and its associations with those occasions is so strong that it is probably best left for them. I include comments on it here as the day-to-day work of a chant choir does include funerals.

Kyrie A

The title at the head of this composition '*Deus genitor almé*' harks back to the days, before definite notation, when the cantors remembered their chants by mnemonics. The syllables of the Latin phrase reminded them in some way of the tune. Indeed in England, before the Protestant Revolution, the words were often sung in elaborately expanded versions of the *Kyrie* not unlike the versions found in the alternative penitential rites in the 1969 *Roman Missal*.

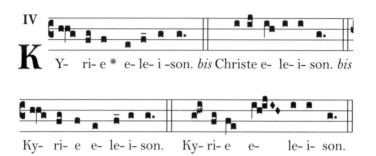

XI. s.

K Y- ri- e * e- le- i -son. *bis* Christe e- le- i- son. *bis*

Ky- ri- e e- le- i- son.   Ky- ri- e   e-   le- i- son.

For those choirs starting out with chant the best way would be to teach this particular composition by rote. In other words, that the conductor sings a phrase to the choir and makes the choir repeat it back. This can be done in cumulative fashion so that the first *Kyrie eleison* is learnt, then the *Christe eleison,* and then the two are put together with the second *Kyrie eleison* (which is the same as the first). Finally, the last phrase is learnt and the whole composition can be assembled. A running sheet for a possible rehearsal is given in Chapter 4.

The choirmaster needs to make special preparation before teaching each chant. This is achieved by a series of questions that should be resolved about each piece. Before he even presents it to the choir he should know the chant well. Thus we would need to know the following in relation to the example:

1. How do we pronounce the text? (see Chapter 5 Latin pronunciation). In this case Kee-ree-ay eh-lay-ee-sohn, Kree-stay, *et cetera*

2. Where are the semitones? In this case between the second line from the top and the space beneath it. Light pencil marking could be useful.

3. What is the structure of the piece when performed? We notice the use of bis and see the following pattern *Kyrie* [repeated] *Christe* [repeated] *Kyrie* (actually a repeat of Kyrie 1) and a final new *Kyrie*.

4. What should the phrasing be? In this case each section of music is quite clear and concise. No breaths should be necessary within each phrase.

5. Who sings what? The cantor commences and sings the first *Kyrie* solo, and then the full choir take up the chant to the end. Alternatively it could be very effective to alternate solo voice with full choir in a performance plan that would look something like this. *Kyrie* (solo), *Kyrie* (full), *Christe* (solo), *Christe* (full), *Kyrie* (solo), *Kyrie* (full).

6. With which notes do we need to take extra care?
   (a) In the opening phrase and its repeat the *horizontal episema* on the note 'le' (in *eleison*) doubles the length of the note.
   (b) Similarly the *quilisma* above 'Ky' in the final *Kyrie* lengthens the first note of the phrase.

Light pencil marking again can be useful here. A circle around a note can be useful especially if the printing is faint or rather small.

Kyrie B

Ad Missam pro defunctis: ?

This second setting of the *Kyrie* found at Mass XVIII is traditionally sung at Requiem Masses. Those of you who know Maurice Duruflé's *Requiem* will immediately recognise the tune. The following notes should be of use in preparing the chant for use:

1. Pronunciation: What was said about *Kyrie A* (above) applies but extra vigilance needs to be taken over the multiple notes (*melisma*) above the vowel 'e'. The vowel sound needs to be constant.

2. Tonality: The 6th mode was popular with late Gregorian composition. The lack of date at the right hand corner was the editor's kind way of saying that the chant really is not that old but because it is popular we will include it. Closest to the modern F major scale (the consistently flattenened note is a dead give away for this mode) a lot of the most popular tunes are written in it, including the Easter alleluia.

3. Structure: We notice the use of bis and see the following pattern *Kyrie* [repeated] *Christe* [repeated] *Kyrie* (actually a repeat of *Kyrie* 1) and a final new *Kyrie*. Common to all phrases is the setting of *eleison*.

4. Phrasing. Two approaches are possible when looking at this melody. Each section consists of two sections which might be likened to a question and answer. In this case the answer is the same throughout (the setting of eleison). If the chant is taken at a reasonable tempo then each section can be sung without a breath. An exception might be made for the final section. Alternatively slight breaks for breath could be made at each quarter bar break.

5. Who sings what? The cantor sings the first *Kyrie* solo and then the full choir take up the chant to the end. Alternatively it could be very effective to alternate solo voice with full choir in a performance plan that would look something like this: *Kyrie* (solo), *Kyrie* (full), *Christe* (solo), *Christe* (full), *Kyrie* (solo), *Kyrie* (full).

6. With which notes do we need to take extra care? The dotted notes directly before each quarter barline need

to be handled carefully so as to not upset the flow of the overall phrase. Thus doubling the length of each note should be immediately followed either by a 'snatch breath' or direct continuation of the chant. The final dotted notes of each section should last two beats with the alternative group/solo taking up the next phrase immediately. The very final syllable can be lengthened three, or perhaps even four times depending on the acoustic of the building.

Sanctus

XIII. s.

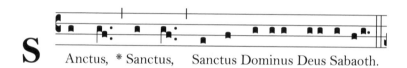

S Anctus, * Sanctus, Sanctus Dominus Deus Sabaoth.

Ple-ni sunt cæ-li et ter-ra glo-ri-a tu-a Ho-sanna in excelsis

Be-ne-dictus qui venit in nomine Domini. Hosanna in excelsis.

1. Pronunciation: Of particular note should be the pronunciation of the word *Sanctus*. Note that the division of syllables should be san-ctus rather than sanc-tus. *Sabaoth* is three syllables, each 'a' should be long, a real 'ahh', and the final syllable is pronounced with a hard t, 'ot'. *Cæli* is 'chaylee', the ch as in 'chair'. Similarly watch out for *excelsis*, 'ek-chayll-seess'. The final 'ni' of *Domini* is frequently mispronounced, it should be 'nee' not 'neh'.

2. Tonality: Note that the editors have not classified this chant into one of the eight modes. This points to the antiquity of the melody which is so simple as to defy classification. The 13th century dating refers to the earliest manuscript that the melody is found in however it is probably much older, indeed it is thought by some to be the oldest chant in common use today.

3. Structure: Broadly, the composition falls into two sections (*Sanctus* and *Benedictus*) each concluding with a *Hosanna*. The melodic material for the *Pleni* and the *Benedictus* are actually variants on each other as is the melodic material for the *Sanctus Dominus* and first *Hosanna*.

4. Phrasing: It seems logical that between the first and second *Sanctus* of the first phrase there should be some separation. Each of the following sections should be sung continuously with single beat breaths at the bar lines.

5. Who sings what? The cantor sings the first *Sanctus* solo and then the whole choir takes up the rest of the chant. If some variation is desired the whole *Benedictus* phrase could be sung by a solo voice with the full choir returning at the final *Hosanna*.

6. With which notes do we need to take extra care? Whilst the quarter bars after each *Sanctus* should be observed this does not mean a tripling of the dotted final note, doubling suffices here as it does on the 'ra' of terra and the 'ctus' of *Benedictus*. Two instances of *liquiescent neumes* (small notes) should be noted, both occur in the final *Hosanna*. These retain a normal note value but in ideal situations should be slightly lighter in tone.

Agnus Dei

XII. s.

A -gnus Dei, * qui tol-lis peccata mun-di: miserere no-bis.

Agnus De-i, * qui tol-lis peccata mun-di: mi-se-re-re no-bis.

Agnus De-i, * qui tol-lis pecca-ta mun-di: do-na no-bis pa-cem.

1. Pronunciation: Particular care needs to be taken with two words; *Agnus* and *miserere*. With the first, note that the syllable break occurs between A and gnus not Ag-nus. The A should be a long 'ahh'. On more than one occasion I have heard a choir start to sound like bleeting with a short 'a' which, although loosely appropriate to the text, is hardly edifying. *Miserere* can be an awkward word to pronounce because of the repetition of 're', and three identical vowels ('e') in a row. The word should be pronounced mee-seh-reh-ray.

2. Tonality: Note that, like the *Sanctus* above, the editors have not classified this chant into one of the eight modes. Again this points to the antiquity of this melody, which has been paired with the *Sanctus* for a very long time. The 12th century dating refers to the earliest manuscript in which the melody is found. Again it is probably much older.

3. Structure: The *Agnus Dei* settings in the *Graduale* have the strongest formal structure to modern ears. Frequently there is direct repetition of the basic melody and here we have it three times without variation. The melody itself can be divided into three sections, an opening clause (*Agnus Dei*), the question (*qui tollis peccata mundi*), and an answer (*miserere nobis*).

4. Phrasing: In practice, the opening clause and question should be sung almost without a break. The answer (*miserere* or *dona nobis*) can be sung after a slight pause, as would the *ora pro nobis* following the name of a saint in a litany.

5. Who sings what? Two approaches seem popular. First the cantor gives out the opening *Agnus* and the choir takes up the rest of the chant. Alternatively, as each of the phrases open with an *Agnus Dei* followed by an asterisk (*) it can be very effective to assign this to a solo voice each time. This makes the connection with the ancient litany form even stronger.

6. With which notes do we need to take extra care? The rule of thumb concerning dotted notes applies here. If the dot appears in the course of the section then double it. At the end of each section a longer lengthening seems desirable. Make the first two final notes (on *nobis*) the same length and the final one (on *pacem*) slightly longer.

Tutorial 2, which appears as Chapter 6, will deal with a simple *Gloria* setting that could be used with Mass XVIII to form a complete set for use on Sundays, solemnities and feast days.

chapter four

REHEARSAL METHODS

Rehearsal techniques for chant are quite different from rehearsing ordinary choral music. Here, more demands are made on the choirmaster, who is obliged to make decisions, preferably in advance, concerning the interpretation of the music employed. This chapter gives some useful guidelines for getting rehearsals on the right track, warnings about some common pitfalls, and a sample rehearsal plan.

Introducing the chant for the first time

The introduction of chant merits some consideration. Currently we are experiencing a considerable resurgence in interest in the chant. The media certainly seems aware of this, at least in Britain and the United States. Chant is not to everyone's taste, indeed you may find some opposition to singing it. This might be based on one of three things: (i) the idea that single line music is in some way inferior music for choirs used to singing part music, (ii) reservations on the basis of liturgical ideas. These are largely misguided and based on poor interpretation of church documents or too much reading of the opinions of local committees on church music. Older members of religious communities will carry a lot of 'baggage' concerning the chant. The loss of it was often very painful and bringing it back seems to make some of them re-live the horrors of the past. (iii) A true dislike of the sound. This seems to have been the case with the Venerable John Henry (Cardinal) Newman, so such an opinion is not without some sensible adherents.

In answer to these objections the following answers might be offered. (i) Single line music sung by a choir in unison, particularly if it is without accompaniment is actually the most difficult music to rehearse and sing properly. Some introduction to the intricacies of preparing a good performance of a chant composition might help them here. (ii) Liturgical objections need to be dealt with very carefully. Anything to do with music can become very emotional, and when dealing with liturgical music questions of faith, obedience, and pastoral responsibilities can confuse the situation. From a literal reading of the documents from, and after, the Second Vatican Council, chant was intended to be preserved even in small churches - it could be argued that chant was made more available to small churches by the publication of the *Graduale Simplex* and the popular English booklet *Jubilate Deo*. The 1960s hang heavily around the shoulders of an older generation. Be gentle with them. (iii) As to the argument on the matter of personal taste there really can be no answer. People holding this opinion are more likely to keep the objections to themselves preferring chant to whatever else might be on offer from the Chamber of Horrors which contains much of that written in the name of good music over the last thirty years.

Chant is probably best introduced to choirs in small doses. Do not attempt to change an established repertoire over night. Start with something which is immediately useful - *Sanctus* XVIII for example (see Chapter 3) - then gradually add to the repertoire. It is important that the quality of the performance really be the best possible, given your resources, from the outset. A badly rehearsed and presented chant, even a simple one, can effectively inoculate a choir and congregation against taking on any more. If the use of Latin is a particular problem (this again is generally restricted to those for whom the 1960s were 'significant') then there are several excellent possibilities. The *Roman Missal* (in the United States the *'Sacramentary'*) has several excellent English chant masses included in them. Material from these could be first introduced as an introduction to the style. Vernacular adaptations are dealt with in Chapter 9.

Preparations - (i) Personal preparation

Much of the success of the introduction of chant can be traced to good preparation on the part of choir directors. In their private preparation - which should double the rehearsal time at least - they should keep the following checklist in mind.

a. Translation
b. Pronunciation
c. Tonality
d. Structure
e. Phrasing
f. Who sings what?
g. 'Problem' notes
h. Tempo [and dynamics]

Each point needs to be carefully considered before they dare step in front of their singers. In practice it is worthwhile making up a sheet of notes for each chant under the checklist headings which can be filed and used in the future. Some may wish to include a copy of the music at the top of the sheet. On the following page is an example sheet based on the material for *Sanctus* XVIII discussed in Chapter 3.

Preparations - (ii) Planning the rehearsal

In practice the time allocated for choir practices is relatively short. This is particularly so in religious communities where other duties are numerous and the choir practice may not be more than fifteen minutes a week with the occasional special rehearsal in preparation for the big feasts. I once thought this was a serious problem but now see that the effective use of short periods of time means that you can get more out of the sometimes unwilling participants if you keep them interested and occupied for the full time set. Always start promptly and never go over the allocated time. The rehearsal time is a contract of honour. Three points for successful chant rehearsals:

(i) Be realistic about the abilities of your singers. Don't attempt to learn one of the Lenten tracts (e.g. *Qui habitat* in *GR* pp.73-76) in a fifteen minute choir practice

Feast of Pentecost   Chant: *Sanctus* XVIII (*GR* pp. 767)

XIII. s.

1. Translation: Holy, Holy, Holy Lord, God of hosts. Heaven and earth are filled with your glory. Hosanna in the highest. Blessed is he who comes in the name of the Lord. Hosanna in the highest.

2. Pronunciation: San-ctus. *Sabaoth* is 3 syllables. *Cæli* is 'chaylee' *excelsis* ('ek-chayll-seess'). The final 'ni' on *Domini* ('nee').

3. Tonality: Not classified. Thought to be the oldest chant in common use. Pitch starting on 'A'.

4. Structure: Broadly, two sections - *Sanctus* and *Benedictus*.

5. Phrasing: 1st and 2nd *Sanctus* separated. Single breath at the bar lines.

6. Who sings what? Cantor sings first *Sanctus* and then full.

7. Warnings: Quarter bars after each *Sanctus*. Doubling same for 'ra' of *terra* and the 'ctus' of *Benedictus*. 2 liquescent neumes in the final *Hosanna*.

8. Tempo & Dynamics: Roughly, metronome marking of punctum = 208. Sanctus **f**, Benedictus **mf**, final *Hosanna* **f**.

Sample checklist for Sanctus XVIII

when your singers have never seen four-line notation. Stick, at first, to what you know they can achieve in a single session. As time goes on you can introduce more complex pieces, perhaps learning them by allocating five minutes of the rehearsal time each week to a 'long term' project.

(ii) The planning of a rehearsal, particularly one with limited time, needs to be very careful. Keep a clock handy and move on to each new section according to the timetable. An example of a fifteen minute rehearsal is given at the end of this chapter.

(iii) Warming up the singers at the beginning of the rehearsal can take just a few minutes. Take a short phrase from the piece you are going to learn and sing it in various pitches gradually getting higher, louder, softer, slower, quicker, using a variety of syllables. This will 'tune' the choir in to singing in unison together. This will make them aware of the three basic qualities needed: good pitch, tone and rhythm.

Three basic concerns

The purpose of the rehearsal is to ensure that all three basic qualities - pitch, tone and rhythm - are in reasonable shape. Perfection is not possible this side of the Second Coming but good results are achievable which may in some way look forward to the singing of the Heavenly host.

The choice of the initial pitch is the responsibility of the choir director. It is the director who should know the abilities and ranges of the voices available and the proper choice of pitch will save time, and tears, in rehearsals. Given the following conservative voice ranges the ideal common pitch range is relatively small.

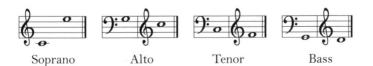

| Soprano | Alto | Tenor | Bass |

Women   Men

In practice, this leaves an octave C-C although extensions by a note or two can be achieved without much grief at the top end of the scale. Trying to extend at the lower end of the scale meets with some problems. These are conservative generalisations and the particular talents of a group of singers would probably produce more optimistic results. Choirs of women religious commonly operate at pitch ranges up to a third (or more) above these generalisations.

The trick is to look at a chant, determine its range, and then find where this could best fit your singers. If we accept a working range of C-D (a ninth) and apply it to the following *Hosanna* then some computation is necessary:

Sanctus XV *GR* p. 762

Ho- san- na   in ex-cel- sis.

The range of this chant (which is the same for the whole of this *Sanctus*) is a major sixth.

do   ti

For reasons of tone quality and text clarity it is generally better to choose the upper end of the pitch range. Because the upper end of the scale is only touched on occasionally it would seem possible to set the upper limit at a 'c #'. Working backwards this would make our starting note an 'f #' and thus the lowest pitch in the excerpt an 'e'.

In transcription this would look like this.

Ho-   sanna   in ex- cel-   sis.

If a chant has an exceptional range (spanning more than an octave) it is possible that the passage was originally meant for a solo voice and you can follow suit.

The second pitch concern that faces the director is the problem of keeping in tune. The most common tendency is to go flat, even when accompanied. However it is not uncommon for trebles to go sharp. Three techniques should be used to help keep the pitch.

(i) Proper breath control: Simply, adequate air is needed to allow the vocal chords to work. Where one breathes during a piece should be negotiated by the director. The preference is always to sing through a phrase but if this is not possible the quarter bars give a good indication of where good deep breaths can be taken.

(ii) Aural exercises: Part of a rehearsal can be given over to small 'games' that encourage remembering the original pitch. Halfway through a phrase get somebody to sing the starting pitch and then play, or sing, what it should be to them. The important thing is to get the choir to be listening for it. Some phrases which repeat a single pitch alternately with decorative material can be used as an exercise in keeping pitch. The following excerpt constantly returns to '*do*'. By getting the choir to concentrate on each return to the 'home pitch' some headway can be made in keeping in tune.

Intende [Offertory] *GR* p. 280

quo-   ni-   am.

(iii) Finally, in an acoustic where there is a lot of reverberation the echo can be deceptive. An echo naturally 'goes flat' as it diminishes. If the choir is listening to the echo to pick up the next note, particularly at the end of a phrase or a verse, gradually the pitch will fall. Again the answer is keeping the original pitch always in mind. I know of one situation where a person was asked to stop singing because they were always going sharp when in fact they were the only singer keeping the pitch!

Opinions as to the right tone of voice for chant vary from place to place. In one place you might find what seems like a whisper, in others a full-throated bellow. Neither seems particularly desirable. For the purposes of singers new to chant, using the same tone is important otherwise a satisfactory blend is not possible. The tone needs to exclude vibrato and the best place to start is a 'natural' voice without any attempt to 'produce' the sound. A wise old choirmaster once likened this to a head voice rather than a throat voice. I tend to liken it to a folk singing voice but this will, of course, vary widely. In solo passages a more produced tone is useful and sometimes a beautiful contrast to the rounder tone of the full choir.

In giving the first guide to singers ask them to imagine that the sound is coming from a cavity inside their heads. It will not be loud at first but will grow in strength with experience. The mouth should be kept rounded but wide enough to imagine a golf ball between the teeth. Finally the air passage needs a straight passage to be used with the greatest economy. Straight backs and upright heads are essential. Sing across the music rather than to it!

When pitch is fine, and tone is under control, rhythm will still be there to plague the director. For practical purposes the following principle could be applied, with apologies to Orwell: 'All notes are equal but some are more equal than others'. Every note should be equal unless some marking lengthens a note. (This has already been detailed in Chapter 2). It is probably helpful to get the singers to keep a constant beat (one beat for each note) going in their heads. This can be achieved by lightly tapping a finger against the book whilst singing, although be careful not to make the resulting chant too wooden or rigid. The mediæval theorists called this beat the *tactus*, probably because of this practice of touch beating against the book.

A particular problem will face those attempting some of the more extended chants. What do you do when multiple repetitions of a note appear above the one syllable? If this is just two or three notes then a simple lengthening of the pitch is called for. However if something like the following appears, drastic action needs to be taken.

Epiphany   *Reges Tharsis* [Offertory] *GR* p. 58.

The first three syllables are not a problem but what are we to do with the 'sis' of *Tharsis*. One might simply lengthen the pitch by eight, however different types of notes are used which suggests some change is needed. Again debate rages over how to execute such passages and the most common resolution has been to slightly reiterate the pitch when the note changes, so in this case the effect in modern notation would be thus however remember that all the pitches on 'sis' are tied and the new notes are just indicating a repercussion (marked by an **x**) which is the technical term for this phenomena.

This sort of repercussion is also called for in passages where a note within repeated notes is distinguished by a *vertical episema*:

Meditabor [Offertory] *GR* pp. 245-246

In this case the repercussion occurs on the note that the *episema* is above or in some cases below. The passage would be executed thus with the repercussion marked by an **x**.

Finally the question of tempo must be considered. No matter what tempo you choose it will always be too fast or too slow for one of your singers. Putting a particular metronome marking forward as a suggestion would be foolish. The tempo really needs to be adapted to the building in which you are singing, to the abilities of the singers, and to the meaning of the text. As a rule of thumb you should select a tempo that will enable the singers to complete short phrases without having to take unnecessary breaths.

Common problems

There are two problems which commonly affect rehearsal practice.

(i) Maintaining interest: Keeping interest in a choir, particularly of religious, is a remarkably hard task. Frequently, despite protestations to the opposite, they just do not want to be there. Human nature being what it is, and clerics awkward characters to boot, you are unlikely to get a straight answer from them about the quality of choir practice that you are running. There will be people in the group who will be against you from the start, and that will not change. The trick is not letting their problems permeate the attitude of the whole choir. An open attitude to choir management is desirable with certain limitations drawn on specifically musical decisions. Extremely troublesome members of choirs tend to absent themselves when they don't get their own way so it is just a matter of waiting.

(ii) The 'bad' voice: If I were to say that there is no such thing as a bad voice and that every voice has the capability of making a musical sound then I think my nose would grow by several feet. It may be pleasant and comforting to say that sort of thing, but it is just not true. Every religious choir director in the world knows this problem, the member who cannot keep pitch or whose voice has no chance of blending. There are two things to remember: (a) It is not their fault. Whilst not born that way, they have acquired a bad use of the voice, and by the time you get to them it might not be possible to correct. (b) What you actually have to do is 'damage control' so as to neutralise the negative effects of the voice. If you are unable to tackle the problem directly then a request to the whole choir can be made to sing softly with key people forewarned to know what this actually means. Professional advice on a particular voice can result in an excellent improvement.

Conducting the chant

The methods used to conduct chant are various. Frequently there will be no conductor in a liturgical context, however in rehearsal clear direction needs to be given by the director to maintain the tempo, and thus the *tactus*, at the same time as giving the appropriate pauses and cues. Anything more expressive than this has no place within the liturgy and should have been prepared before hand.

Giving the signs in a clear manner is essential. A wavering fluttering hand doing impersonations of a pre-bagged grouse is of little use. The basic act of conducting is pointing to events and there must be a clear point in the air which is that point of reference. A single hand suffices. Joining the thumb and first finger, surely

33

not a totally forgotten art for clerics, gives the hand a focus point. The joined digits form the pointing stick that places the beat or the emphasis in the air. The gesture made can be just pointing to the spot in the air. Other gestures will be needed to bring phrases off (make a small circle in the air) and to hold the final note. If the pitch is going flat point upwards with your index finger. If the choir is too loud, a flat extended hand making a patting movement can calm well meant but frenetic efforts.

One should presume that the choir can keep the constant pulse by themselves and that your job is actually to make emphasis. In a composition such as the *Agnus Dei* of Mass XVIII we might make the following conducting chart.

XII. s.

A -gnus Dei, * qui tol-lis peccata mun-di: miserere no-bis. *Bis*

Agnus De-i, * qui tol-lis pecca-ta mun-di: do-na no-bis pa-cem.

Here the **x** indicates the basic pulse and o the circular terminating sign. At first, when preparing scores for practices, it will be useful to make similar style markings as well as how long you intend to lengthen the notes at the ends of phrases and what sort of break between phrases you have in mind. All should be calculated against the basic beat (the *tactus*).

With practice you will develop your own style of conducting the chant which is effective for the group with which you work. Do not be scared to ask their opinions. Am I clear enough? Could it be done better in any way? What if I tried this? The two basic principles are this; simplicity and clarity. Don't over-conduct and make sure everybody knows what your hand signs mean.

A sample rehearsal

Time allocation: 15 minutes. **08.30–08.45**
Task: *Kyrie A* from Mass XVIII (*GR* pp. 767–768) (see below)
Preparations: personal and sufficient copies of the music already in
the singers' places.

Running sheet.

08.25 Meet with the cantor [and accompanist]. Explain the task
for today's rehearsal. Give them the pitch on which the chant
will be sung. In this case starting on 'A'.

08.30 Warm up using the following phrase from the *Kyrie*:

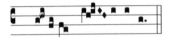

Start on an 'E' and repeat it going up a semitone at a time
using the vowel 'ahh'. Repeat the exercise using the syllable
'ee', then 'oh'. Thus:

1. Ahh   Ahh
2. Ee   Ee
3. Oh   Oh

1. Ahh   Ahh
2. Ee   Ee
3. Oh   Oh

The exercise should be done rather quietly at first (say **mp**).
If there is time you can then practice getting louder or
softer but in warm up rehearsals keep between **p** and **mf**.

08.35 Explain what will be done in the rehearsal, learning the
Kyrie from Mass XVIII, and a bit about the piece, especially
pointing out the repetitions of the first two phrases. Then

---

the cantor can sing the first phrase, and the full choir can repeat it:

Ky- ri- e e- le- i- son.

Note the lengthening of the 'le' in *eleison*, doubling the note value, and point out the other notes in this piece which are to be lengthened.

Then repeat the process for the other phrases. The learning process should be quicker each time. Remind them that the final phrase is the same as the warming-up exercise you did at the beginning of the rehearsal.

08.40 Explain how the *Kyrie* will be sung i.e. cantor-full, cantor-full, cantor-full and explain that there will be a full beat between each phrase.

Check if there are any questions.

Sing the whole *Kyrie*. If there is time do it a second time, by now they should have memorised a good part of it and you can encourage them to look at you during the rehearsal to follow your beat and direction.

XI. s.

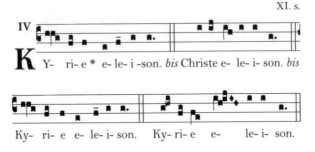

K Y- ri- e * e- le- i -son. *bis* Christe e- le- i- son. *bis*

Ky- ri- e e- le- i- son. Ky- ri- e e- le- i- son.

08.45 Thank everybody, and tell them what you will be looking at next rehearsal, suggesting, if they have time, that they might like to have a look at it before then.

Some problems that you come across might be solved by looking at the frequently asked questions at the end of this book.

chapter five

LATIN PRONUNCIATION

A gain we hit upon a topic about which one is supposed to have opinions. The ideal for the singing of chant in the Catholic Church was the *more Romano,* that is, in the Roman manner. This was a standard set down at the beginning of the 20th century, influenced largely by international conferences on the singing of chant, and possibly by the growing need to standardise Latin pronunciation amongst those using it daily either for curial or liturgical purposes. Of course where one stops and the other starts is a moot point. Nevertheless the pronunciation of Latin for the chant is undoubtedly different from any of the theories proposed for Classical Latin. Compare any two recordings of the same piece and you will find pronunciations varying according to national accents. What follows is one possible approach.

The following is adopted from the *Liber Usualis.*

Vowels

a	is pronounced *"ahh"*	as in	"father"
e	...	*"e"* (short) ...	"bed"
i		*"ee"*	"been"
o		*"or"*	"Lord"
u		*"oo"*	"soon"
j		*"ee"*	"been"

Diphthongs

ae, oe	both pronounced *more Romano* like 'i' above, however English pronunciation commonly renders them as 'ay'
au, eu, ay	whilst technically one syllable, the second vowel is 'hinted' at. See *Liber Usualis*, p. xxxvij.
ei	two syllables, unless in the word *hei* when the vowels are separated.
ui	before "q" or "ng" is one syllable, but in the form "ui" (as in *cui*) is two syllables.

With any other doubled vowels both letters are pronounced separately.

Consonants

c	is pronounced	"*k*"	as in	"cart" except as below
d	...	"*d*"	...	"dog"
f		"*f*"		"father"
g		"*g*"		"guide" except as below
h		silent		except "*mihi*" and "*nihil*" where it is pronounced "*ch*" as in the Scottish "lo*ch*"
l		"*l*"		"long"
m		"*m*"		"moon"
n		"*n*"		"noon"
p		"*p*"		"pet"
q		"*kw*"		"queen"
r		"*r*"		"red"
s		"*s*"		"salt"
t		"*t*"		"table"
ti and		"*tsee*"		when followed by a vowel preceded by any letter except "s", "x", and "t"

v	is pronounced	"*v*"	as in	"vegetable"
x	...	"*ksh*"	...	before "e", "æ", "oe", "i", "y"
	or	"*ksc*"		before "a", "o", "u"
y		"*ee*"		same as "j", see *vowels*
z		"*dz*"		

Consonant variations

c	before "e", "ae", "oe", "i", "y" is "ch" as in	"*ch*urch"
cc	before "e", "ae", "oe", "i", "y" is "t-ch"	*ecce* is "et-che"
sc	before "e", "ae", "oe", "i", "y" is "sh" as in	"*sh*ed"
ch	is pronounced "k"	
g	before "e", "ae", "oe", "i", "y" is soft as in	"*g*enius"
gn	is soft as in	"sig*n*or"
th	is pronounced "t" as in	"*th*omas"

With any doubled consonant ["bb", "nn", "ll" *et cetera*] both letters are pronounced separately.

Pronunciation guide for Mass

(i) Kyrie

LATIN	PHONETIC PRONUNCIATION	TRANSLATION
Kyrie eleison.	*Keereeay ehlayeesohn.*	Lord, have mercy.
Christe eleison.	*Kreestay ehlayeesohn.*	Christ, have mercy.
Kyrie eleison.	*Keereeay ehlayeesohn.*	Lord, have mercy.

39

(ii) Gloria

LATIN	PHONETIC PRONUNCIATION	TRANSLATION
Gloria in excelsis Deo	*Gloreeah een ekschayllsees Day-oh*	Glory to God in the highest.
et in terra pax hominibus bonæ voluntatis.	*et een terrah parks hormeeneeboos bohnay voloontahtees.*	And on earth peace to men of good will.
Laudamus te.	*Lowdahmoos tay.*	We praise you.
Benedicimus te.	*Baynaydeecheemoos tay.*	We bless you.
Adoramus te.	*Ahdoorahmoos tay.*	We worship you.
Glorificamus te.	*Glooreefeecahmoos tay.*	We glorify you.
Gratias agimus tibi propter magnam gloriam tuam.	*Grahtseeahs ahhgeemoos teebee proptehr mahgnam glooreeahm tooahm.*	We give you thanks for your great glory,
Domine Deus, Rex cœlestis, Deus Pater omnipotens.	*Dohmeenay Dayoos, Rex chaylestees, Dayoos Pahtehr omneepotens.*	O Lord God, heavenly King, God the Father almighty.
Domine Fili unigenite, Jesu Christe.	*Dohmeenay Feelee ooneegeneetay, Yehsoo Kreestay.*	Lord Jesus Christ, the Only-begotten Son.
Domine Deus, Agnus Dei, Filius Patris.	*Dohmeenay Dayoos, Ahgnoos Dayee, Feeleeoos Pahtrees.*	Lord God, Lamb of God, Son of the Father
Qui tollis peccata mundi, miserere nobis.	*Kwee tollees peckahtah moondee, meesehrehray nohbees.*	Who takes away the sins of the world, have mercy on us.
Qui tollis peccata mundi, suscipe deprecationem nostram.	*Kwee tollees peckahtah moondee, soosheepay daypraykahtseeonem nostrahm.*	Who takes away the sins of the world, receive our prayer.
Qui sedes ad dexteram Patris, miserere nobis.	*Kwee saydays ahd dekstehrahm Pahtrees, meesehrehray nohbees.*	Who sits at the right hand of the Father, have mercy on us.
Quoniam tu solus Sanctus.	*Kwohneeahm too sohloos Sanktoos.*	For you alone art holy;
Tu solus Dominus.	*Too sohloos Dohmeenoos.*	you alone art Lord;
Tu solus Altissimus, Jesu Christe.	*Too sohloos Ahlteesseemoos, Yehsoo Kreestay.*	you alone, O Jesus Christ,
Cum Sancto Spiritu, in gloria Dei Patris.	*Coom Sahnkto Speereetoo, een glooreeah Dayee Pahtrees.*	together with the Holy Spirit, are most high in the Glory of God the Father.
Amen.	*Ahmen*	Amen.

(iii) Credo

LATIN	PHONETIC PRONUNCIATION	TRANSLATION
Credo in unum Deum,	*Kraydoh een oonoom Dayoom,*	I believe in one God,
Patrem omnipotentem, factorem caeli et terrae, visibilium omnium, et invisibilium.	*Pahtrem omneepotehntehm, factorehm chaylee et terray, veeseebeeleeoom omneeooom, et eenveeseebeeleeoom.*	the Father Almighty, Maker of heaven and earth, and of all things visible and invisible.
Et in unum Dominum Jesum Christum, Filium Dei unigenitum.	*Et een oonoom Dohmeenoom Yehsoom Kreestoom, Feeleeoom Dayee ooneegeneetoom.*	And in one Lord, Jesus Christ, the Only-begotten Son of God,
Et ex Patre natum ante omnia saecula.	*Et eks Pahtray nahtoom ahntay omneeah saykoolah*	born of the Father before all ages;
Deum de Deo, lumen de lumine, Deum verum de Deo vero.	*Dayoom day Dayoh, loomen day loomeenay, Dayoom vehroom day Dayoh vehreoh.*	God of God, Light of Light, true God of true God;
Genitum, non factum, consubstantialem Patri: per quem omnia facta sunt.	*Jeneetoom, non fahktoom, consoobstahntseeahlem Pahtree: pehr kwem omneeah fahktah soont.*	begotten, not made; of one substance with the Father, by whom all things were made.
Qui propter nos homines, et propter nostram salutem descendit de coelis.	*Kwee prohptehr nohs ohmeenays, et prohptehr nohstrahm sahlootem dayshendeet day chaylees.*	Who for us men, and for our salvation, came down from heaven.
ET INCARNATUS EST DE SPIRITU SANCTO EX MARIA VIRGINE: ET HOMO FACTUS EST.	*Et eenkahrnahtoos est day Speereetoo Sahnktoh eks Mahreeah veergeenay: et ohmoh fahktus est.*	AND WAS INCARNATE BY THE HOLY GHOST OF THE VIRGIN MARY, AND WAS MADE MAN.
Crucifixus etiam pro nobis, sub Pontio Pilato passus, et sepultus est.	*Kroocheefeeksoos etseeahm proh nohbees, soob Pohntseeoh Peelahtoh pahsoos, et sehpooltoos est.*	He was also crucified for us, suffered under Pontius Pilate, and was buried.
Et resurrexit tertia die, secundum Scripturas.	*Et rehsoorreksit tehrtseeah deeay, saycoondoom Skreeptoorahs.*	And on the third day He rose again according to the Scriptures,
Et ascendit in coelum: sedet ad dexteram Patris.	*Et ahshendeet een chayloom: saydet ahd dekstehrahm Pahtrees.*	and ascended into heaven. He sits at the right hand of the Father:

LATIN	PHONETIC PRONUNCIATION	TRANSLATION
Et iterum venturus est cum gloria, judicare vivos et mortuos: cujus regni non erit finis.	*Et eetehroom vehntooroos est coom glohreeah, yoodeecahray veevohs et moortoo-ohs: kuyoos raygnee non ehreet feenees.*	and He shall come again with glory, to judge the living and the dead: and His kingdom shall have no end.
Et in Spiritum Sanctum, Dominum et vivificantem: qui ex Patre Filioque procedit.	*Et een Speereetoom Sahnktoom, Dohmeenoom et veeveefee-cahntehm: kwee eks Pahtray Feeleeohkway prohchaydeet.*	And in the Holy Spirit, the Lord and Giver of life, Who proceeds from the Father and the Son,
Qui cum Patre et Filio simul adoratur, et conglorificatur: qui locutus est per prophetas.	*Kwee coom Pahtray et Feeleeoh seemool ahdoorahtoor et cohnglohreefeecahtoor: kwee lohcootoos est pehr Prohfaytahs.*	Who, together with the Father and the Son, is adored and glorified: who spoke through the prophets.
Et unam, sanctam, catholicam et apostolicam Ecclesiam.	*Et oonahm sahnktahm, kahtoleekahm et ahpostohleekahm Ayklayseeahm.*	And one, holy, Catholic, and Apostolic Church.
Confiteor unum baptisma in remissionem peccatorum.	*Kohnfeetayoor oonoom bahpteesmah een raymeesseeohnehm pehkkahtohroom.*	I confess one baptism for the forgiveness of sins.
Et exspecto resurrectionem mortuorum.	*Et ekspektoh Raysoorrektseeohnehm moortoo-ohroom.*	And I await the resurrection of the dead
Et vitam venturi saeculi.	*Et veetahm vehntooree saykoolee.*	and the life of the world to come.
Amen.	*Ahh-men.*	Amen.

(iv) Sanctus-Benedictus

Sanctus, Sanctus, Sanctus, Dominus Deus Sabaoth.	*Sahnktoos, Sahnktoos, Sahnktoos, Dohmeenoos Dayoos Sahbahoht.*	Holy, holy, holy Lord God of Hosts.
Pleni sunt coeli et terra gloria tua.	*Playnee soont chaylee et tehrrah glooreeah tooah.*	Heaven and earth are filled with your glory.
Hosanna in excelsis.	*Osahnnah een ekschayllsees.*	Hosanna in the highest.
Benedictus qui venit in nomine Domini.	*Baynaydeektoos kwee vayneet een nokmeenay Dohmeenee,*	Blessed is He Who comes in the Name of the Lord.
Hosanna in excelsis.	*Osahnnah een ekschayllsees.*	Hosanna in the highest.

42

(v) Agnus Dei

LATIN	PHONETIC PRONUNCIATION	TRANSLATION
Agnus Dei, qui tollis peccata mundi: miserere nobis.	*Ahgnoos Dayee, kwee tollees peckahtah moondee meesehrehray nohbees.*	Lamb of God, Who takes away the sins of the world, have mercy on us.
Agnus Dei, qui tollis peccata mundi: miserere nobis.	*Ahgnoos Dayee, kwee tollees peckahtah moondee meesehrehray nohbees.*	Lamb of God, Who takes away the sins of the world, have mercy on us.
Agnus Dei, qui tollis peccata mundi: dona nobis pacem.	*Ahgnoos Dayee, kwee tollees peckahtah moondee: dohnah nohbees pahchehm*	Lamb of God, Who takes away the sins of the world, grant us peace.

chapter six

TUTORIAL 2: GLORIA XV

The *Gloria* from the Mass setting *Dominator Deus* (numbered XV in the *Graduale*) forms a good partner to the other parts of the ordinary of the Mass found in Mass XVIII. Whilst *Missa de Angelis* (Mass VIII) is well-known by an older generation I think the *Gloria* of this Mass has several distinct advantages. (i) Like *Missa de Angelis* it is based on repetitive phrases. (ii) Its range does not exceed a sixth and for all but one note, at the end, it stays within a fifth. (iii) It does not have many awkward *melismas*. (iv) Its short repetitive units provide an excellent example of the rhythmic implications that need to be 'decoded' from the chant text. This makes it one of the most useful compositions within the *Gradual*. With such a small range, transposition for almost any situation is possible. This may make it sound like the worst tune available but it maintains interest, for the singer and the listener, through some very clever tricks in the rhythm.

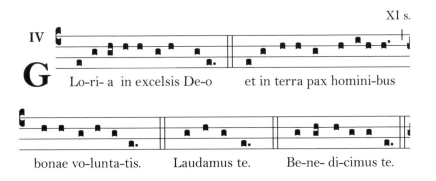

Ado-ramus te.   Glo-ri-fi-camus te.   Gra-ti-as a-gimus ti-bi

propter magnam glo-ri-am tu-am.   Domi-ne De-us, Rex caelestis,

De-us Pa-ter omni-pot-ens.   Do-mi-ne Fi-li uni-ge-ni-te,   Je-su.

Christe   Domi-ne De-us,   A- gnus De-i,   Fi-li-us Patris.

Qui tol-lis pecca-ta mundi,   mi-se-re-re no-bis.   Qui tol-lis

pecca-ta mundi,   susci-pe depre-ca-ti-o-nem no-stram.   Qui

se-des ad dexte-ram Patris,   mi-se-re-re nobis.   Quo-ni-am tu.

so-lus sanctus   Tu so-lus Domi-nus.   Tu so-lus Altissimus,

46

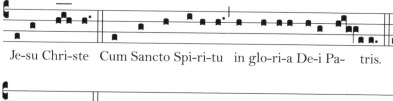

Je-su Chri-ste   Cum Sancto Spi-ri-tu   in glo-ri-a De-i Pa-   tris.

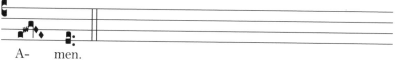

A-   men.

Pronunciation

Particular care of the enunciation needs to be taken in this Gloria as the distinctive rhythmic qualities of the composition often 'bounce' off the distinct finality of the consonants. In rehearsal slight emphasis needs to be made on the 't' of *te* at the ends of phrases, and the ends of phrases needs to have a clear pronunciation of final consonants. 'S' needs to be exactly that, not an ongoing 'sssss' but something that really terminates the word and stops the rhythm 'in its tracks'. The same might be said for 'm'. When a vowel ends a phrase, such as 'e' it needs to retain its quality but not its duration beyond the written value.

Tonality

Gloria XV, like many ancient compositions, has a remarkably small range extending across a fifth but with an extension, in the very last phrase ('*Amen*'), down one tone. Thus we have the following data:

Mode IV has strong implications in modern tonality and it is easy to view it as a cross between 'e' and 'a' minor. Commencing the chant on an 'e' would be practically possible and, when accompanied, quite satisfactory. However in practice the chant will go flat, except with the most accomplished of choirs, and commencing the chant a semitone higher, on an 'f' will keep it within the optimum range and avoid problems that flattening would cause on the final *Amen.* Thus the intonation in modern notation could look like this:

Glo- ri- a   in excel-sis De-o

The final *Amen* merits special attention because the tonality of mode IV has been used here explicitly to emphasise the finality of the word. Not only does the *Gloria* operate within a relatively small range but only certain notes of the mode are used. In particular '*fa*', written on the second line from the bottom, is avoided until the very final phrase.

fa

A- men.

In an otherwise pentatonic (five-note) melody we have the sudden intrusion of a semitone. This note also has an uneasy relationship with the highest note of the composition. The two form a tritone (augmented 4th, diminished 5th), what the mediæval theorists called *diabolus in musica* - the 'devil in music'. A combination of this semitone within its phrase (i.e. the *Amen*) and the relationship with the highest note of the composition make this note stand out giving an extra colouring and finality to the phrase. The practical point is this: care needs to be taken to make sure this is sung as a true semitone. There will be a tendency to try and widen it towards a full tone which will only weaken the rather beautiful effect it has.

Structure

Some of the greatest compositions in Western art music are made up of relatively small and simple units which are varied to form a total composition. Often the listener is unaware that this is going on and only becomes aware with greater familiarity with the piece. Five basic 'themes' make up the piece, they are shown opposite.

[*Group 1 Use of the 'full' theme*]

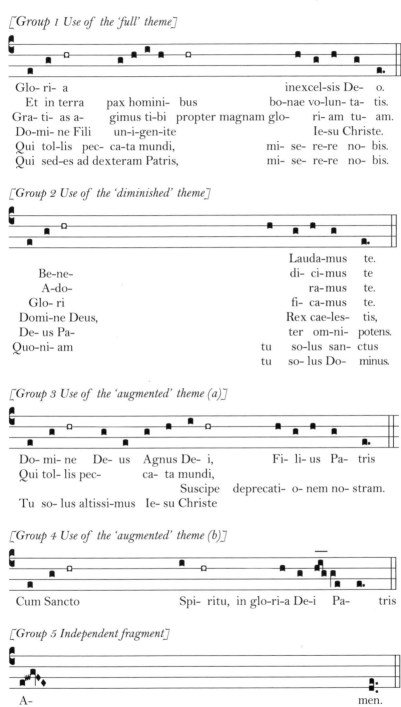

Glo- ri- a   inexcel-sis De-   o.
Et in terra   pax homini- bus   bo-nae vo-lun- ta- tis.
Gra- ti- as a-   gimus ti-bi propter magnam glo-   ri- am tu- am.
Do-mi- ne Fili   un-i-gen-ite   Ie-su Christe.
Qui tol-lis pec- ca-ta mundi,   mi- se- re-re no- bis.
Qui sed-es ad dexteram Patris,   mi- se- re-re no- bis.

[*Group 2 Use of the 'diminished' theme*]

                              Lauda-mus   te.
Be-ne-   di- ci-mus   te.
A-do-   ra-mus   te.
Glo- ri   fi- ca-mus   te.
Domi-ne Deus,   Rex cae-les-   tis,
De- us Pa-   ter om-ni- potens.
Quo-ni- am   tu   so-lus san- ctus
                      tu   so- lus Do- minus.

[*Group 3 Use of the 'augmented' theme (a)*]

Do- mi- ne   De- us Agnus De- i,   Fi- li- us Pa- tris
Qui tol- lis pec-   ca- ta mundi,
                  Suscipe   deprecati- o- nem no- stram.
Tu so- lus altissi-mus Ie- su Christe

[*Group 4 Use of the 'augmented' theme (b)*]

Cum Sancto   Spi- ritu, in glo-ri-a De-i   Pa-   tris

[*Group 5 Independent fragment*]

A-   men.

In rehearsal the most interesting of these groups are 3 and 4. Here the material is varied for the sake of the text. By these emphases they reveal a picture of the world view in which this chant originated: an emphasis on the 'Lord God' (*Domine Deus*) who is the 'Lamb of God' (*Agnus Dei* - the repetition of the phrase is strong), who will take away the 'sins of the world' (*peccata mundi*) and 'receive our prayers'(*suscipe*). In Group 4 we see the decorative emphasis on the Fatherhood of God (*Patris*) in a phrase outlining the ordinary range of the composition by downward steps of a third.

Phrasing

All the phrasing of *Gloria* XV is remarkably short and can be easily executed in single breaths. It is important to notice the strong use of an 'arch' form in each phrase. There is the definite feel of a question and answer and this should be made clear to the singers. Without wanting to give too much emphasis to the dynamic possibilities here it could be useful to keep in the back of one's mind a rising and falling of the phrases almost like waves coming in and going out at the beach.

Who sings what?

This aquatic analogy can be extended as there appears to be two currents operating with the waves washing over each other. This can be made clearer by allocating the individual 'verses' to alternating groups. Customarily the singing of the *Gloria* is divided between two groups. The priest gives out the opening phrase and this is taken up (*Et in terra*) by a small group who then sing alternate phrases with the full choir for the rest of the piece. The divisions are indicated by the double bar lines. Finally, all come together for the *Amen*. The intervals that begin and end each phrase form, at least to the modern ear, consonance rather than dissonance. This feature can be exploited. With careful practice a slight overlapping of the phrases can be extraordinarily effective. On the lengthening of each final note the next phrase can commence keeping the rhythm going and creating the beautiful effect of implied harmonies.

'Problem' notes

Three items need to be pointed out in rehearsal. Firstly the lengthened notes that occur in this piece should be simply doubled. Particular attention needs to be made to those occurring within phrases so that they do not get excessively lengthened. The presence of quarter bars must be taken as a guideline not an indication of a longer pause between sections.

Towards the end of the piece the following triple lengthening occurs.

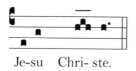

Je-su   Chri- ste.

The group of three above the 'Chri' of *Christe* is the problem. This occurs relatively frequently at the ends of phrases. Should we follow the rules set out in Chapter 2 and double each note equally so that we have a total of 6 beats on the syllable? This is the solution followed in many places. However a rather enchanting effect is achieved if they are interpreted as a 'triplet' (3 beats stretched into the space of four) against the duple *tactus*. The reason for this 'judgement call' on the part of some choir directors is a matter of interpretation of the original notation that lies behind the chant. Some believe that the extended *horizontal episema* (in this case across three notes) indicated a break in the tactus - a slowing down to emphasise a word. The *tactus* returned to normal 'tempo' at the end of the group.

The *quilisma* on the final *Amen* needs to be explained, particularly if the group of singers is new to the chant. The problem of keeping the proper value of the phrase and the slight slowing down natural to the end of such a long chant can be confusing at first. Strict conducting is probably needed here:

A- men.

Tempo [and dynamics]

    Gloria XV is an extremely well designed and functional composition designed to get the liturgical job done with a minimum of fuss. It seems unnecessary to make any complex dynamic or tempo directions. The contrast created by the two forces (small group or cantor versus full choir) give it sufficient colour. The full choir should aim at **mf** or at most **f** during its sections.

chapter seven

GENRE
antiphons, psalms, hymns, other forms

This chapter concerns the different types of chant material with which the director needs to be familiar. Whilst possessing a common modality, which give the particular sound to the music, and whilst the rhythmic principles remain basically the same, there are some distinguishing features that will affect the approach to rehearsing and performing them.

This is not the place for a dissertation on the history of the liturgy, however, along with each of these genres, three classifications need to be defined which do not affect the structure of the music but refer to its use: *Ferial* material is for the ordinary days of the year, the *Common* provides sets of hymns, antiphons *et alia* which are classified by type of saint (apostle, martyr, bishop, virgin *et cetera*) and the *Sanctoral*, or Proper of Saints, describes material specific to a particular saint or feast. Liturgical books generally have these three sections.

Antiphons

(i) A short to medium length composition designed to be sung before and after another text, commonly a psalm. The text might be drawn from the psalm itself or from a feast day, might be a free composition drawing on the writings of the saint or recalling their particular virtues and deeds. Generally, the more important the day the more complex the antiphon. Antiphons are found in the Divine Office on the psalms and the canticles and in Mass they form the basic 'response' of the Introit, Gradual, Offertory and Communion chants.

(ii) The great Marian antiphons ('Salve Regina' *et alia*) once conformed to the above pattern but have since come to be sung without their psalm. A few other chants have a similar history. The Communion chants at Mass, whilst technically possessing psalm verses, rarely use them.

Psalms

Psalms are the backbone of the Divine Office and are always present in the liturgy of the Mass. Formal practical advice needs to be sought when first approaching the use of psalms. No matter how much you read in books there are niceties and tricks that are just not explained. The best policy is to approach a choir director who has some experience with psalm singing and get them to teach you. What follows here are some simple suggestions.

The problem: You are confronted with an antiphon with indications that certain psalm verses should be sung between repetitions of the antiphon.

Antiphon at the Vigil for the Dead

[Luke 23.42 + Psalm 22 *GR* pp. 679]

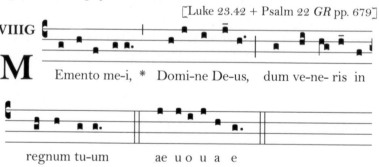

1. *Do-mi*-nus pascit me, et nihil mihi **dee**rit: * in pascuis virentibus me *col-lo*-**ca**vit.

2. *Super* aquas quietis e**du**xit me, * animam me*am* re*fe*cit
   …

The antiphon itself is written out in full. Above the capital letter at the beginning is given the tone and its ending that the psalm verses should be sung to. As an *aide memoire*, the final part of chant (its ending) is written above the vowels of the final syllables of the *Gloria Patri* (sae-cu-lo-rum. A-men). Below the antiphon are written the psalm verses (just two verses of Psalm 22 are shown here). Often the first verse is written out in full so there can be no doubt:

Do-*mi*-nus pascit me, et nihil mihi **de**-e-rit: * in pa-scu-is

vi-renti-bus me *col-lo-***ca**- vit.

Summarising the tone (viiiG) then we can see that it has three basic parts; a beginning (the intonation), middle (the mediation) and end (the ending). Occasionally, when the first half of a psalm verse is in two distinct clauses, a division is made called the flex which is indicated by a '✝'. In between these points is the reciting note symbolised by the transparent note. We can summarise the basic form of the chant like this:

Intonation   Flex   Mediation   Ending

Various systems of pointing the psalms (that is marking or varying the print of the text) have been attempted to give a guide as to where the various parts of the chant come during the text. Older editions may just have acute or grave accents above the stressed syllables, others have nothing at all, expecting the singer to know Latin well enough to know where the stresses come. This is not the reality of today, well not yet, and the system used in the illustrations above is used in the *Graduale Romanum* and other contemporary books. Comparison between the basic chant form and the verse written out in full reveals that whenever part of the text is altered by italicisation or bolding some movement from the reciting note occurs. The intonation is not always used however, generally it is used with chants during Mass and for the Gospel Canticles at Lauds (the *Benedictus*) and Vespers (the *Magnificat*).

If you are presenting a choir with psalm verses for the first time it is probably wise to write them out in full. If the Latin accents are not clear even the most experienced of singers have difficulties, and in practice often prepare 'cheat sheets' to help themselves out.

On occasion you will find the instruction '*et non repetitur in psalmis*' (not repeated in the psalm). This occurs when the antiphon text is a direct quote of a full, or substantial, verse of a psalm. On rare occasions (such as Psalm 109) this can alter the psalm tone slightly and it is then written out in full.

Remembering the principle of equal notes the question of all those syllables on the one reciting note must be addressed. In an ideal world all the syllables on the reciting note should be sung equally. Similarly the notes of the intonation should have the same value. A slight slackening off is common at the flex and the ending but the tempo must return with the very next note. Dom Alphège Shebbeare wrote that each psalm verse contains two types of singing: on the recitation notes we speak the notes at a pitch but at the mediation and the ending we sing the words and notes.

The speed of recitation can be the cause of some misery unless ground rules are laid down from the start. It would seem sensible that the basic tempo should be slightly slower than we would normally speak the text and certainly at a speed at which the speakers can clearly pronounce each word without the affectation of a dramatic recitation. The basic rule is that all must sing together. If syllables are not sung together then the overall rhythm of the chant is undermined by the 'machine-gun' effect of syllables ricocheting around the building. Whilst antiphons should not be dragged they should be sung slightly slower than the psalm verses. The space between antiphon and the beginning of the psalm, or the end of the *Gloria Patri* and the return of the antiphon, is longer and should be carefully rehearsed.

56

Hymns

Hymns belong largely to the Divine Office however there are two occasions when they form an integral part of the Mass liturgy; (i) on Maundy Thursday during the Procession to the Altar of Repose (and for other Eucharistic processions) and (ii) associated with the anointing and vesting of the new priest in the rite of Ordination.

Other chants are given the title hymn more from a lack of being able to describe them in any other way. The basic characteristic is this: metrical music regularly repeated against a changing text which itself has a distinct and repetitive rhythm. Two things to be remembered about hymns: (i) the tempo remains the same throughout except for a slight slowing down on the final Amen. (ii) The space between the verses needs to be considered. If you have assigned alternate verses to different groups then there needs to be a pause twice the length of the ordinary pause before the final verse, commonly a *doxology*. This is to allow the group that has just completed its assigned verse to get a full breath before everybody sings together.

Canticles

Texts from the Bible, but not from the Psalter, are included amongst the psalms in the Divine Office and Easter Vigil. These are treated exactly as psalms. Three canticles (all from the Gospels) receive special treatment because of their liturgical prominence. These are the *Benedictus* (at Lauds) the *Magnificat* (at Vespers) and the *Nunc Dimittis* (at Compline). Their execution is basically the same as the psalms, however, to give them a greater prominence, the intonation is included at the beginning of each verse of the canticle. Solemn forms of the tones also exist for each of the eight modes and the advice of an expert should be sought before attempting them. They are not compulsory but can add a certain extra elegance to a feast if well-handled.

Readings

The liturgical chant books provide tones for the recitation of the readings at Mass and the Divine Office. These tone formularies operate with the same principles as those given for the use of psalm tones, however the symbols used are less standardised. In addition to these simple tones there are more complex and extended recitatives which border on a genre of their own. Among these we might list the Passions, Reproaches, and Lamentations of Holy Week, and the *Exultet* sung at the Easter Vigil. Each of these special recitatives is written out in full in the liturgical books.

As almost all of this liturgical recitative is solo work the use of an experienced tutor is to be highly recommended. A plain direct style is to be recommended and the histrionics associated with much professional singing avoided. An 'objective' approach is worthy of these sacred texts. The most common simple chant used is that for the Gospel and new deacons, indeed more experienced clergy, could do with some practice on this. *The Graduale Romanum* (pp. 805-808) gives three options, the first of which is the easiest.

Full stop   Question   End

The *Roman Missal* and the *Sacramentary* give several options for the singing of the lessons in the vernacular. Similarly, provision is made for the singing of the various prayers of the Mass. (See Chapter 9).

Dialogue chants

The final category we should note is that of functional chants that get business done quickly. These are the dialogues between minister and people, the most common of which is the salutation *Dominus vobiscum* and its response *et cum spiritu tuo*. Again, simplicity is the key. The theatrical should be avoided and an elegant objectivity encouraged.

chapter eight

ACCOMPANIMENT

If one were being truthful, then one would have to admit that there is something exceedingly attractive about chant sung well and unaccompanied. At the other end of the scale there is something exceedingly awful about chant being accompanied and yet sung badly. As good as it can be without, the day-to-day reality is that there are times when the chant will be accompanied. Some basic principles need to be laid down so that when it is there it supports the singing rather than detracting from it.

To accompany or not accompany

For	Against
1. Accompanying is a practice approved, at least implicitly, by the Church.	1. The chant by its monodic nature eschews any accompaniment.
2. Modern ears can only hear the modality in terms of modern tonality.	2. The modality implied by the chant cannot be realised on modern instruments
3. Modern harmony can support modal melodies without significant damage.	3. Modern harmony ruins the modality behind the very structure.
4. The performance of the chant is not static and accompaniment may be considered part of a living tradition	4. The chant must be returned to the pristine purity of its original performance style.

I am sure that there are more arguments for and against but if we realise that the contemporary situation really makes this a matter of personal preference and taste then only one real concern remains. If one is to use accompaniment then the modality of the chant, essential to its structure and meaning, must be reflected, protected and supported. The following is very much an introduction, the books cited in Further Reading should be of further use.

Antiphons

Simplicity is the ruling quality of all chant accompaniment and this is particularly so in the accompaniment of the antiphons which are the core 'free composed' material of the repertoire. Here we find frequent repetition of material, phrases that are shared between one antiphon and another, and the range of chords needed is really relatively small particularly in the shorter examples. Two possible accompaniments come to mind for the following:

[*Monastic Antiphonale* p. 151.]

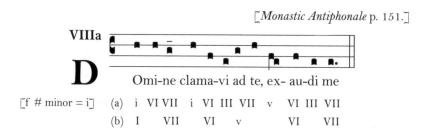

[f # minor = i] (a) i VI VII i VI III VII v VI III VII
                 (b) I   VII   VI   v   VI   VII

The chords suggested in line (a) are certainly possible but are too much for the small structure. The quality of the chant lies in the careful use of *melisma* to outline the meaning of the text and the arches that form each of its phrases. These are simple risings and fallings and accompaniment (a) would seem to be distracting from the simple structure. Accompaniment (b) simply supports and acknowledges where 'questions and answers' have commenced and finished. It probably errs on the side of complexity.

Psalms

The starting point for learning good accompaniment are the psalms themselves. Simplicity again is the key but much will be learnt by improvising on the tones. By experimentation, the multiple possibilities of simple harmonies can be discovered. Particularly, use of different inversions, and changes between minor and major chords, can be extraordinarily effective whilst maintaining a basic familiar harmony that lends support to the singers. The following are some of the possibilities for Dom Gregory Murray's Tone I which he devised for vernacular psalm singing;

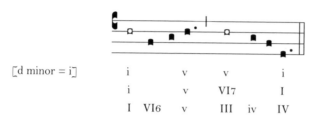

[d minor = i]

		i		v	v		i
		i		v	VI7		I
	I	VI6		v	III	iv	IV

Like antiphons the psalm tones should be examined for their 'significant moments' - the intonations, flexes, mediations and endings - and the choice of chord movement should reflect these points.

Hymns

When reasonable confidence has been achieved with the psalm tones the hymns of the Divine Office can offer a wealth of learning particularly in experimenting with varied accompaniments between the alternating verses. The accompaniments offered in many good hymn books should be studied and imitated particularly in the subtle movements of the inner voices. What can be a boring elongation of a single chord can be transformed by such changes. The temptation to over ornament should be avoided. Hymn accompaniments, like other chant accompaniments, need to be prepared in advance. An example of the chord pattern of a typical office hymn with a possible registration is given at the end of this chapter.

Learning

Learn from the masters. If you can't find a living one to give you help search the second-hand book shop for the books of prepared accompaniments that used to be on every organ console in Christendom. Of particular value are the books produced by Dom Desrocquettes of Quarr Abbey. These are out of print but can be found. The *Liber Cantualis* has an accompaniment edition by Henri Potiron which demonstrates the value of simplicity and subtle changes.

Registration

Which instruments can be used? Certainly the pipe organ is the traditional and favoured instrument for the accompanying of chant however other instruments were undoubtedly used in the past (see Chapter 10). In choosing instruments and in the choice of organ registration two essential qualities must be available, adequate support for the vocal line and the ability to support rather than confuse the rhythmic impetus. For this reason essentially percussive instruments, like the piano, are less successful.

Again the basic principle is simplicity. Foundation stops are the best, add colour from string stops rather than reeds or mutations. The pedal 16' tone will be found very useful in keeping the pitch in full choir sections. If problems occur in solo passages the addition of a 4', or the slight opening of the swell, should return the erring singers to the proper pitch.

Tune in Winter VIII   [*Lucis Creator optime: AM* pp. 128-129]

Intonation (swell)   Basic registration
                                          Great: Soft 8' coupled to swell
                                                      Swell: Soft 8'+4'
                                          Pedal: Soft 16' coupled to swell

First verse

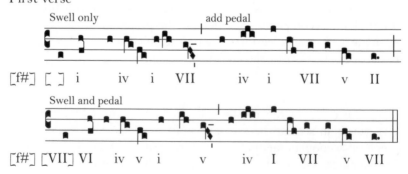

For verses (1, 3, 5......) using a solo voice, or small group, swell (and pedal) should be sufficient. For full choir verses (2, 4,.... and the doxology) the great with pedal should be used.

chapter nine

VERNACULAR ADAPTATIONS

This chapter deserves a book in its own right. Indeed when Father Percy Jones wrote his *English in the Liturgy* some thirty years ago he was working in the right direction and provided some excellent examples which found their way into the published missals after 1970. Unfortunately, the book was largely ignored. Jones' presumption that some chants (but not all) could be adapted to vernacular texts met with dismay from two groups: (i) Chant purists who were so blinded by the presumption that chant sprung from the Latin text that an adaptation was impossible. (ii) Iconoclasts who wanted to remove any connection with the artistic values or language of the past. The less said about this latter group the better, save that the mortality of the human condition will, without doubt, take care of this attitude within a few decades.

To adapt or not to adapt

Two questions need to be addressed. Firstly are we causing some sort of artistic travesty of earth-shattering consequence if we adapt the chant to a vernacular text? Do we debase the very art form itself by making such a radical change? Secondly, what are the benefits in vernacular adaptations? Are there any good reasons for adapting instead of employing good quality new composition?

The question of artistic travesty is complex, however it can be resolved in the negative on purely historical evidence. The chants in the published texts have a long history and not all of that history was in the Latin language. Double language chants still exist in the *Improperia* for Good Friday, indeed the *Kyrie Eleison* is an admittedly latinised, Greek composition. Behind the psalm tones there is a history longer than the liturgical use of Latin (*Tonus Peregrinus* is almost identical to a Sepphardic tone) and within the Latin corpus itself there is continual adaptation and borrowing. Whilst we are not surprised to find a single melody adapted to fit the texts of the 'O' antiphons it is more surprising to discover the same tune adapted for the Common of Doctors (*O Doctor Optime*). The relatively small body of *Alleluia* verses show that the process of adaptation was very much part of the Gregorian tradition.

As to the language question (Are Latin and English so different in stress systems that they cannot share a music?) we come to a value judgement. Much of this argument against vernacular adaptation presumes that a certain pronunciation and stressing of Latin is the only correct method and therefore a language without these characteristics cannot carry the chant. This argument has some strengths, however, it misses the point. Yes there are problems, indeed we might say that it is impossible to sing Latin chant in English but it is possible to adapt it so that an English text can use chant melodies. The purists will scream that this is not Gregorian Chant. Fine! What is more important is that there is a musical language with certain strengths that is available and should not be ignored when enriching vernacular liturgies.

Direct adaptations

Direct adaptations seek to transcribe existing chant melodies to new texts. There is a long tradition of this in English church music, the most activity occurring at the turn of the 20th century and continuing up till the 1950s. Publications are numerous and can be found frequently in second-hand book shops. The finest of these adaptations, edited by Dr Palmer, were published by St Mary's Wantage. They are, in their own way, quite unique because Palmer did not use Roman liturgical books as the basis for his chants but rather those of the Sarum Use that dominated England before the Protestant Revolution. Occasionally Palmer alters the musical line to fit the English text. For those interested in vernacular adaptation the Palmer settings serve principally as a guide to what is possible.

The office hymns, and to a lesser degree the psalm tones, are quite useable. The antiphons, however, are considerably distant from contemporary English.

Free adaptations

Free adaptations of the chant appeared hot on the tail of the Protestant liturgical books in 1549. John Merbecke's *Book of Common Prayer Noted* is one of the earliest and finest examples of a systematic adaptation to a new modern language. In more recent years there have been adaptations according to Merbecke's principles (one note to a syllable), notably by Richard Proux. Here the chant background is clear, particular chants are even evident, but the words of the new translations have been considered for modern stress and the melodies adapted to fit. Examples of this style of adaptation are found in the English language *Roman Missal* and *Sacramentary*.

Neo-Gregorian composition

There is a long tradition in composition of taking Gregorian formulas as a base and then composing anew. Earlier in the century Beatus Ruyser provided simple chants for some of the key ceremonies of the year where the traditional chants offered too many difficulties to be learnt quickly and performed accurately. This in itself continued a tradition of Gregorian style composition from the 18th century. Many of the most popular of chants (*Salve Mater, Puer Nobis* et alia) belong to this category, indeed several items in the *Kyriale* seem to belong to this category.

Such style of composition can teach us a lot. An example of the use of the style could be useful in preparing new material, in the vernacular, for choirs. In Chapter 6 we saw an analysis of *Gloria* XV which highlighted the very kernel of the piece. Using this as a model, a totally new vernacular *Gloria* could be created, using Dom Gregory Murray's Tone 1 as a basis:

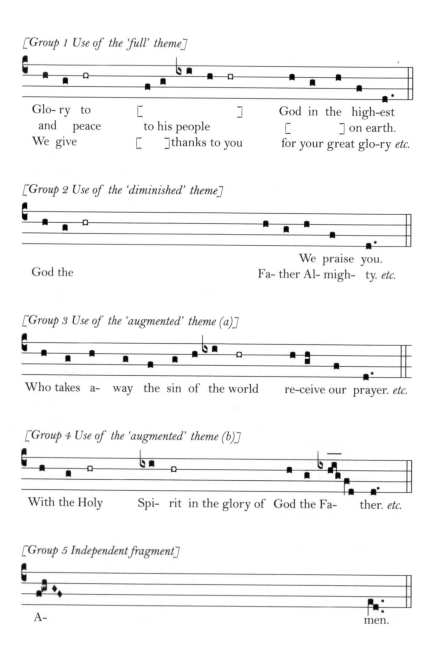

[Group 1 Use of the 'full' theme]

Glo- ry to   [   ]   God in the high-est
and peace   to his people   [   ] on earth.
We give   [   ]thanks to you   for your great glo-ry etc.

[Group 2 Use of the 'diminished' theme]

We praise you.
God the   Fa- ther Al- migh- ty. etc.

[Group 3 Use of the 'augmented' theme (a)]

Who takes a- way the sin of the world   re-ceive our prayer. etc.

[Group 4 Use of the 'augmented' theme (b)]

With the Holy   Spi- rit in the glory of God the Fa-   ther. etc.

[Group 5 Independent fragment]

A-   men.

Modal composition

The modality of the chant itself has been the inspiration for much music outside the liturgical field. Given the fact that the modal system offers a considerably wider range of possibilities than the major-minor system, whilst at the same time being so much more natural to the physiology of the human voice, it is somewhat surprising that contemporary liturgical composers have been somewhat slow to use a tonality which has been such a rich source for everybody from the symphonist to the jazz pianist within the last century.

A new body of liturgical composition is now appearing and volumes such as *Hymns for Prayer and Praise* have an excellent selection of arranged Gregorian hymn tunes and totally new compositions in modal style.

Conclusions

This chapter has been included because there are occasions when the best way of introducing a group to chant proper is through vernacular adaptation especially if there are lingering doubts about the use of Latin. Whilst this is a problem that will not last for long it is a sensitivity that should be observed for the sake of long-term goals. When looking at a vernacular adaptation the relationship between the text and the music must be carefully examined to ensure that the natural flow of the words is not being distorted by a straight jacket approach to matching the old music with the new words. Any composition which places *melisma* on insignificant words or syllables should be avoided. As a rule of thumb, the simpler the approach the better.

Dom Gregory Murray prepared a series of eight tones corresponding to each of the 8 modes which have stood the last thirty years well. As they do not seem to have been published together before they are included below. They could form the basis for new compositions, the psalms are easily sung to them and they are simple enough to be applied to other texts.

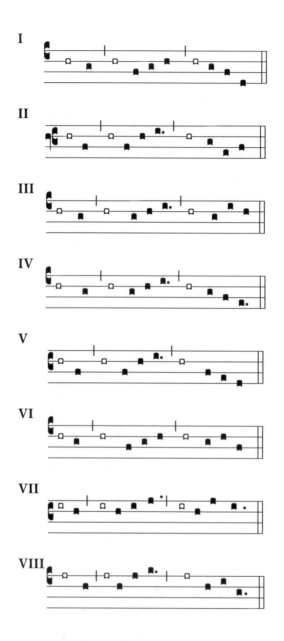

*Dom Gregory Murray's eight tones,
corresponding to the eight modes*

chapter ten

FREQUENTLY ASKED QUESTIONS

This chapter summarises some of the material of the previous chapters and answers a few particular questions that arise from particular situations.

Introduction

Why is there a revival in chant singing at the moment?

By the time you read this, the popular enthusiasm for chant may well have waned. The incredible success of the recordings from Santo Domingo de Silos and the knock-on effect for the recording industry has been surprising. All successful products fulfil a need and the current spiritual vacuum is being felt by those even without any particular faith. For some, the 'spirituality' of the chant seems to fill that need.

Who is singing chant?

The most common place you can still hear chant is in monasteries and convents. In England some of the finest singing can be heard at Quarr Abbey and St Cecilia's Abbey on the Isle of Wight. Good vernacular adaptations can be heard at Mount Saint Bernard, near Leicester, and modern modal music can be heard at Belmont Abbey near Hereford. This is only a handful of around 40 religious houses using chant in Britain. The new Office is sung daily at Westminster Cathedral. Evensong in the Anglican Cathedrals and Colleges often includes chant both in Latin and English. A society which promotes chant performance exists. It is the Gregorian Association. (London, England: Information from Mr. G. MaCartney, 26 The Grove, Ealing, London, W5 5LH, UK.)

Historical

Has not the Church banned the use of Gregorian Chant?

The argument runs something like this: As the Church has banned Latin therefore we can't sing Gregorian Chant. This is pure ignorance. Neither Latin nor chant was banned at the Second Vatican Council. Rather indeed their use was encouraged and pastors of parishes were required to arrange for their congregations to know at least the simplest chants and the basic parts of the Mass in Latin.

What is the correct way of singing the chant?

There is no single correct way of singing the chant. Numerous theories and methods are proposed, the most popular derives from the work of the monks of Solesmes, but after observing the basic rules it is up to the Choir Director to set rules that suit the local situation.

Who first invented the chant?

The origins of chant are mysterious, however, we can make an educated guess that the tonal system developed in the first few Christian centuries drawing on numerous ancient sources. The first codification of the chant was under Pope Saint Gregory the Great which has given the style the popular name 'Gregorian'.

What are the official books of chant?

The official books of chant are the *Graduale Romanum* and the *Antiphonale Romanum*. Certain other books contain special chants but so far only the Passions have been officially released. Most of the special chants associated with Holy Week will be found in the *Missale Romanum*. For monasteries following the Rule of Saint Benedict the *Antiphonale Monasticum* remains in use. Elements of this have been revised according to the principles in the *Thesaurus Monasticum* and have been published as the *Psalterium Monasticum* and the *Liber*

Hymnarius. Liturgical books for the Mozarabic and Ambrosian Rites are also being revised.

Notation

Why are there only four-lines?

Gregorian four-line notation is sort of half way along the timeline in the history of music-writing. The earliest writing had no lines, then just a single line, and gradually four were found the most useful. There were experiments as far as ten but these were too difficult to read and ended up split into two groups of five giving the modern system of staves and staffs.

What is a neume?

A neume is a note or group of notes in Gregorian notation expressing a particular musical gesture. A table of the most common neumes with their transcriptions is included in Appendix 2.

How do I tell where the semitones are?

With Gregorian clefs, the first semitone is always between the line the clef rests on and the space immediately below. Other semitones may occur depending on the position of the clef.

Can a note be altered in pitch?

It is possible for a note to be flattened by a semitone with the flat sign. This returns to normal after the end of the word or a bar line, whichever comes first. Very rarely the pitch will be corrected to normal by a modern natural sign.

Can a note be altered in length?

Lengthenings are certainly possible. The most common is the dot after the note or the note with a horizontal episema above it. Certain other lengthenings occur the details of which may be found in Chapter 2.

Rehearsal methods

What is the ideal rehearsal?

The ideal rehearsal has specific aims to be realistically achieved within the time allocated. Each rehearsal should include a brief warm up period and an explanation of the particular problems that the chant has. It is important to stay within the given time limits. A sample rehearsal is outlined in Chapter 4.

How do I manage with limited time?

Careful time management needs to be used. Something positive can be achieved within the most limited time. The trick is not to set unreasonable goals for the rehearsal. A complete *Gloria*, for example, cannot be learnt anew in five minutes. However, particular problems with that *Gloria* can be addressed. When starting to teach chant it is important that the singers know they are achieving something. Start with short pieces that can be completely taught within the given time.

How do I manage with limited singers?

Again this is a matter of careful planning. Choose chants that are within your singers' capabilities and make use of the stronger singers for more complex music. Sometimes complicated passages can be given to solo voices and used that way until the singers are ready to learn it.

What do I do with the bad voice?

Problem voices do exist, particularly in monastic choirs where singers are not always voluntary. Some experimentation is needed and perhaps some personal coaching if that is possible. The important thing is to create a situation where the voice does not do damage to the rest of the texture. Assigning a smaller group of singers to passages that prove problematic is an ancient tradition on which we can rely in difficult times.

Latin pronunciation

Can you explain the difference between Classical and Ecclesiastical Latin?

In pronunciation this is basically a question of Latin as an academic language and Latin as a living language. In vocabulary Ecclesiastical Latin incorporates many borrowed words from Greek and Hebrew and occasionally other languages. In recent times totally new words have been devised to convey concepts and objects not known in either the Classical or Medieval periods.

How do you pronounce the following difficult words?

Problem words in the Ordinary of the Mass can be checked in Chapter 5. Other common words that can cause difficulties are 'mihi' (*meekee*), 'euge' (*yoojay* or even *ay-yoojay*) and 'ecce' (*etchay* or even *ekchay*).

Genre

What is the difference between the different genres of chant?

There are four genres: (i) Free compositions with their own rhythmic patterns, (ii) Formulas which use a melodic fragment and apply it to a prose text (such as the psalms), (iii) Metrical compositions which have a regular repeated melody and rhythm (such as hymns) and (iv) Recitatives, where a prose text (for example the Exultet or a Lesson) are sung to a developed formula chant.

Why do some antiphons have verses and others not?

Theoretically all antiphons had verses at one time. By the twentieth century only the Introits retained their verses (taken from the psalms). In current usage appropriate verses can be added to extend the length of a particular movement to cover the liturgical action.

Accompaniment

Should I accompany the chant?

Ideally the answer is no. In reality it is a matter of custom and need. If your singers need the support of an organ to keep them at pitch then use it. If they keep on going flat or sharp despite the organ then it is better to do it unaccompanied.

What stops should I use?

Chant accompaniment should be transparent really leaving the melody at the forefront. 8' stops are ideal with 4' for extra support. The use of a pedal 16' can help the pitch remain stable in 'full' choir sections.

Must we use the pipe organ?

Whilst the organ has stood the test of time and is the favoured instrument for accompanying, the mediæval performers used a wider variety of instruments including the dulcimer, harps, and even the equivalent of brass instruments. A decision would have to be made on the basis of local resources and taste.

Where can I find accompaniments written out?

At the time of writing most books of accompaniments are 'out of print'. A search of second-hand book shops can net some real gems and some absolute horrors. The *Liber Cantualis* is still available from Solesmes and contains simple modal accompaniments by Henri Potiron. For more information on this book, and others from Solesmes, see the Further Reading section. If you can find them the books edited by Dom Desrocquettes are particularly instructive.

Vernacular adaptations

What are the main problems in adopting chant into English?

The main problem in adopting chant is the matching of English word stress to music designed for the equal syllables of Ecclesiastical Latin. Care needs to be taken that the melody does not make the vernacular seem ridiculous or forced. In setting the psalms it is perhaps better to use simplified versions of the tones.

Is there a simple way of starting to chant in English?

The Psalter is the basis for all Christian song, and a good introduction to the sound of chant could be in the use of simple tones set to the psalm texts (see Chapter 9). The Office hymns reproduced in places such as *The English Hymnal, The New English Hymnal* and *Hymns for Prayer and Praise* would be the next step combining the new modality and style with the familiar regularity of versified hymns. Then you can move on to antiphons and the other types.

Additional Questions

Are there courses I can attend in Gregorian Chant?

There are several courses available. A full academic programme is available in chant at the Pontifical Institute of Music in Rome. Several Universities and colleges offer courses in chant as part of a Sacred Music Course and the University of Limerick offers an MA in chant performance. Short courses are taught by the Schola Gregoriana in Cambridge, the Gregorian Schola in Sydney and numerous places in the United States often attached to monasteries. Day sessions have been offered by the Panel of Monastic Musicians, the Royal School of Church Music and the Gregorian Association in Britain. Diocesan music officers should be aware of such courses.

Where do I find individual teachers?

It is possible and desirable to get individual tuition in chant. The best way is probably to attend a day course and approach the course leader during the day. Monasteries are often willing for people to come and experience the chant on site and have discussions with the choir director. An approach needs to be made to the Superior of the monastery concerned and some financial offering made for their troubles.

Are there good published 'methods' that I could buy?

Most older books of chant contain an introduction on how to sing it. A particularly fine introduction can be found in *Plainsong for Schools* and the English rubric edition of the *Liber Usualis* has a more detailed description. Of extended published courses Mrs Justine Ward's *Gregorian Chant* (Washington: Catholic Education Service, 1923) is almost without peer. It is unfortunately out of print, however, an excellent exposition of Mrs Ward's teaching has now appeared prepared by Professor Theodore Marier (*Gregorian Chant Practicum based on Music Fourth Year - Gregorian Chant by Justine Bayard Ward*, Washington: Catholic University of America Press, 1990) at the Catholic University of America.

THE MODES

The first thing that must be noted about chant modality is that it is a theoretical method of explaining the tonality of the repertoire. Admittedly it is a very ancient system of explanation but the melodies revealed and restored over the last century frequently do not fit the modal descriptions demanded by the medieval theorists. The origins of the system seem to be in the desire to fit the chant into the theoretical writings of some classical writers of antiquity that became available around the time that a preponderance of theorising commenced.

Full descriptions of the modes may be found in the books by Hiley and Apel, see Further Reading. Writings concerned with modal accompaniment often have insights into the actual workings of modal tonality. Most primers contain tables illustrating the modes. The following is a transcription based on Apel and Hiley.

	Final	Scale	Theoretical Descriptions	Modern 'Starting Note'
1	d		Dorian *Protus Authenticus*	
2	d		Hypodorian *Protus Plagalis*	
3	e		Phrygian *Deuterus Authenticus*	
4	e		Hypophrygian *Deuterus Plagalis*	
5	f		Lydian *Tritus Authenticus*	
6	f		Hypolydian *Tritus Plagalis*	
7	g		Mixolydian *Tetrardus Authenticus*	
8	g		Hypermixolydian *Tetradus Plagalis*	

appendix two

TABLE OF TRANSCRIBED NEUMES

Notation	Name	Transcription
One Note		
	Punctum	
	Rhombus	
	Virga	
Two Notes		
	Podatus or Pes	
	Clivis	
Three Notes		
	Torculus	
	Scandicus	
	Scandicus	
	Scandicus	
	Porrectus	
	Climacus	
	Climacus	
	Salicus	

Note that the transcriptions are presented at a variety of transpositions to demonstrate the freedom of the notation style.

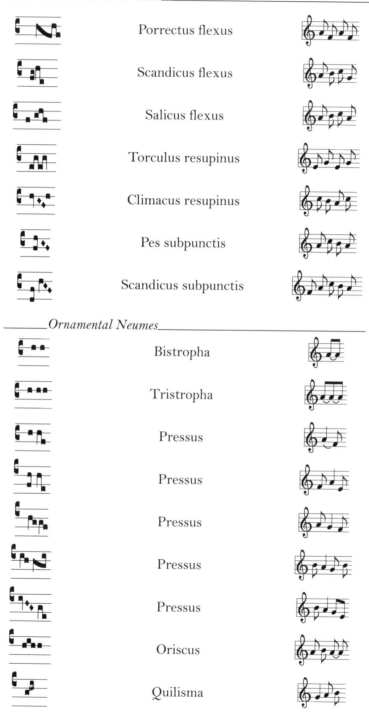

Porrectus flexus

Scandicus flexus

Salicus flexus

Torculus resupinus

Climacus resupinus

Pes subpunctis

Scandicus subpunctis

Ornamental Neumes

Bistropha

Tristropha

Pressus

Pressus

Pressus

Pressus

Pressus

Oriscus

Quilisma

appendix three

THE RHYTHMIC CONTROVERSY

Throughout this book reference has been made to the problems associated with the rhythm of the chant. This appendix summarises the basic positions taken at the moment.

Two basic positions are common each with subdivisions. Both derive from fundamental differences in opinion about the way the early neumes should be interpreted and transcribed:

(i) The Rhythmic position: This argues that essentially all notes are equal unless some additional consideration lengthens the note. All neumes therefore are composed of multiples of one and all may be broken down into combinations of 2 beats and 1 beat. This is essentially the presupposition behind the Solesmes Method. Exponents: Mocquereau, Gajard, Ward. Pothier's position is ambiguous. Cardine`s semiological approach allows for great variation from the basic principle.

(ii) The Mensuralist position: This argues that the neumes may be interpreted with varying lengths and are therefore unequal. The complexity of the various systems of transcription proposed means that there are multiple interpretations possible. Multiply this by the possibility that the value of the neumes changed over the centuries and the combinations are legion. Exponents: Wagner, Vollaerts, Murray, Houdard, Riemann, Dechevrens, Fleury *et alia.*

GLOSSARY

æuouae	The vowel sounds within the Gloria Patri (q.v.) written at the end of an antiphon (q.v.) to indicate the placing of the termination (q.v.) in a psalm tone (q.v.). Representing the words sæculorum Amen.
Agnus Dei	Part of the Ordinary (q.v.) of the Mass sung before the priest's communion.
Alleluia	Part of the Proper (q.v.) of the Mass sung before the Gospel.
Ambrosian	Liturgical rite proper to Milan with significant structural differences to the Roman Rite. The Gloria from the chant repertoire is included in the *Graduale Romanum*.
antiphon	The basic free composition form in chant. Originally designed to emphasise the theme of the text it surrounded in later times the form came to stand on its own as well.
Antiphonale	A collection of hymns and chants for the day hours of the Divine Office.
Benedictus	(i) Part of the Ordinary (q.v.) of the Mass sung with the Sanctus at the end of the Preface and before the Canon (Eucharistic Prayer) (ii) The Gospel canticle (q.v.) at the end of Lauds.
Beneventan	Chant repertoire associated with the south of Italy possibly closely related to Old Roman chant. (q.v.)
bis	A direction appearing at the end of a phrase indicating that it should be sung twice. Occasionally appearing in older books as '*ii*' or even '*ij*'.
bistropha	neume *See Appendix 2*
canticle	(i) The Gospel canticles occur at the end of the Divine Office. These are the *Benedictus* (q.v.) (Lauds) the *Magnificat* (q.v.) (Vespers) and the *Nunc Dimittis* (q.v.) (Compline). (ii) Other canticles derived from the Old Testament and New Testament occur in the Office of Lauds from time to time with the psalmody.

climacus	neume *See Appendix 2*
climacus resupinus	neume *See Appendix 2*
clivis	neume *See Appendix 2*
common	A section of the liturgical books containing generic propers (q.v.) appropriate to a variety of saints or occasions.
Communion	Part of the Ordinary (q.v.) of the Mass sung during the communion of the people.
Credo	Part of the Ordinary (q.v.) of the Mass sung after the homily on Sundays and feasts.
custos	Small guiding note appearing at the end of a line of music to indicate the pitch that the next line commences with.
Deuterus Authenticus	3rd mode (*see Appendix 1*) also described as Phrygian.
Deuterus Plagalis	4th mode (*see Appendix 1*) also described as Hypophrygian
diabolus in musica	The tritone or augmented 4th so called because of its acoustical harshness and the theoretical difficulties it proposed to the ancient writers on chant.
diamond *punctum*	neume = *rhombus. See Appendix 2*
Dorian	1st mode (*see Appendix 1*) also described as *Protus Authenticus.*
doxology	The final verse of an office hymn (q.v.) containing an ascription of glory to the Trinity.
ending	The final section of a psalm tone (q.v.) often indicated by the letters æuouae (q.v.) at the end of an antiphon.
episema	(i) a horizontal line introduced in the Solesmes method to indicate some desired lengthening of a note. (ii) a vertical line indicating the position of the *ictus* (q.v.)
Exultet	The extended prose chant sung by the deacon at the blessing of the Paschal Candle during the Easter Vigil.
feria	The ordinary days of the year without feast.
flex	A variation in the first half of the psalm tone (q.v.) to allow for an extended text.

formularies	Melodic fragments which can be applied to a variety of texts.
Gloria	Part of the Ordinary (q.v.) of the Mass sung in the introductory rites on Sundays and feasts except in Advent and Lent.
Gloria Patri	Sung at the end of psalms and canticles in (q.v.) the Divine Office and appearing also at the introduction to each Office.
Gradual	Part of the Proper (q.v.) of the Mass sung between the lessons.
Graduale	A liturgical book containing the Proper (q.v.) and Ordinary (q.v.) chants for Mass.
Hosanna	Part of the Ordinary (q.v.) of the Mass sung within the *Sanctus* and *Benedictus* at the end of the Preface and before the Canon (Eucharistic Prayer)
Hymnale	A liturgical book containing the Office hymns (q.v.) for the Divine Office.
Hypermixolydian	8th mode (*see Appendix 1*) also described as Tetradus Plagalis.
Hypodorian	2nd mode (*see Appendix 1*) also described as Protus Plagalis.
Hypolydian	6th mode (*see Appendix 1*) also described as Tritus Plagalis.
Hypophrygian	4th mode (*see Appendix 1*) also described as Deuterus Plagalis.
ictus	In the Solesmes method a rhythmic characteristic of the chant indicated by a small vertical episema and associated with the method's concept of the verbal rhythm of Latin.
Improperia	The extended prose chant sung in Greek and Latin at the Veneration of the Cross on Good Friday.
intonation	The opening formula of a psalm tone (q.v.).
Introit	Part of the Proper (q.v.) of the Mass sung at the entry of the priest and ministers.
Invitatory	The opening psalm (94) and its antiphon at the Office of Matins (Vigils/Readings)

jubilus	Extended melisma on a single syllable found at the end of *Alleluia* verses before the final return of the *Alleluia*.
Kyriale	A liturgical book containing the chants for the ordinary (q.v.) of the Mass. Normally bound together with the *Graduale* (q.v.).
Kyrie	Part of the Ordinary (q.v.) of the Mass sung during the introductory rites.
Liber Hymnarius	A liturgical book containing the Office hymns (q.v.) and Invitatories (q.v.) for the Divine Office.
Liquescent	The diminution of a note within a neume to indicate its function as terminating the word.
Lydian	5th mode (*see Appendix 1*) also described as *Tritus Authenticus*.
Magnificat	The Gospel canticle (q.v.) at the end of Vespers.
Mediation	The change of pitch at the end of the first half of a psalm verse.
Melisma	The setting of multiple notes to a single syllable. In the Gregorian repertoire this can extend beyond 20 notes.
Mensural	The performance approach to chant which holds that the proper transcription of the manuscripts reveals unequal note values between the neumes. See Appendix 3.
Missale	A liturgical book containing the texts necessary for the priest at Mass as well as the chants pertaining to his role.
Mixolydian	7th mode (*see Appendix 1*) also described as Tetradus Authenticus.
monodic	Single line music, i.e. without accompaniment or other parts.
Mozarabic	Liturgical rite and chant repertoire proper to parts of Spain. The chant repertoire remains largely undeciphered.
Neo-Gregorian	Chant compositions written since the 19th century Gregorian revival in imitation of the earlier compositions.
neume	The basic building block of a phrase of chant. The basic neumes are tabulated in Appendix 2. (*adj.* neumatic).

Nunc Dimmittis	The Gospel canticle (q.v.) at the end of Compline in the Roman rite.
Offertory	Part of the Proper (q.v.) of the Mass sung during the preparation of the bread and wine to be consecrated during the Eucharistic prayer.
Office Hymn	Metrical and versified compositions sung during the Divine Office concentrating on the theme of the day.
Old Roman	Chant repertoire which preceded and overlapped the Gregorian repertoire in Rome.
Ordinary	The 'invariable' sung portions of the Mass; Kyrie, Gloria, Credo, Sanctus-Benedictus, Agnus Dei. (q.v.)
oriscus	neume *See Appendix 2*
pes subpunctis	neume *See Appendix 2*
pes	neume *See Appendix 2*
Phrygian	3rd mode (*see Appendix 1*) also described as Deuterus Authenticus.
podatus	neume *See Appendix 2*
porrectus flexus	neume *See Appendix 2*
porrectus	neume *See Appendix 2*
pressus	neume *See Appendix 2*
Proper	The variable portions of the Mass: Introit, Gradual, Tract, Alleluia, Sequence, Offertory, Communion, Post Communion. (q.v.)
Protus Authenticus	1st mode (*see Appendix 1*) also described as Dorian.
Protus Plagalis	2nd mode (*see Appendix 1*) also described as Hypodorian
psalm tone	A melodic formula containing and intonation (flex), mediation and ending for the singing of psalms and canticles during the Divine Office and the verses of the Proper (q.v.) at Mass.
punctum	neume *See Appendix 2*
quilisma	neume *See Appendix 2*
registration	The choice of stops in organ accompaniment.

rhombus	neume *See Appendix 2*
Rhythmic	An approach to interpreting the rhythm of chant which presumes that all notes are equal but some are more equal than others. *See Appendix 3.*
Sacramentary	A liturgical book containing the texts necessary for the priest at Mass as well as the chants pertaining to his role. In America the vernacular adaptation of the Missale (q.v.).
Sanctoral	A section of the liturgical books containing the chants proper to a particular saint or feast.
salicus flexus	neume *See Appendix 2*
salicus	neume *See Appendix 2*
Sanctus	Part of the Ordinary (q.v.) of the Mass sung with the Benedictus at the end of the Preface and at the beginning of the Canon (Eucharistic prayer).
Sarum	Liturgical use dominant in Britain until the Reformation. The chant repertoire possesses significant variants.
scandicus flexus	neume *See Appendix 2*
scandicus subpunctis	neume *See Appendix 2*
scandicus	neume *See Appendix 2*
Semiology	The study of the original meaning of the neumes (q.v.) in their earliest forms.
Sepphardic	Chant proper to synagogues in Spain and the Middle East.
tactus	The underlying and continual beat beneath the rhythm of the chant.
Tetradus Authenticus	7th mode (*see Appendix 1*) also described as Mixolydian.
Tetradus Plagalis	8th mode (*see Appendix 1*) also described as Hypermixolydian.
Tonus Peregrinus	The 'wandering tone' so called because the reciting note of the second half is lower than that of the first.
torculus resupinus	neume *See Appendix 2*

torculus	neume *See Appendix 2*
Tract	Part of the Proper (q.v.) of the Mass sung between the readings, and replacing the Gradual during Lent.
trebles	Boys who sing the top line(s) of a composition.
tristropha	neume. *See Appendix 2*
tritone	The *diabolus in musica* or augmented 4th so called because of the theoretical difficulties it proposed to the ancient writers on chant.
Tritus Authenticus	5th mode (*see Appendix 1*) also described as Lydian.
Tritus Plagalis	6th mode (*see Appendix 1*) also described as Hypolydian.
vernacular	Adaptations of the official liturgical texts into local languages.
virga	neume *See Appendix 2*

FURTHER READING

Liturgical books

Missale Romanum (Vatican, Typis Polyglottis Vaticanus. 2002)

The official Mass Book of the Roman Rite, this large and expensive altar tome contains the chant for the Eucharistic Prayers, most prefaces and other chants which occur in the ordinary of the Mass.

Graduale Romanum (Solesmes. 1974)

Contains the Mass chants (introits, graduals, tracts alleluias, offertories, communions and sequences) of the liturgical year. The Kyriale is also included, containing gregorian settings of the Kyrie, gloria, credo, sanctus and agnus Dei. Another edition of the Graduale is the graduale triplex (solesmes 1979). The triplex is critical edition of the graduale, with neums in their ancient forms printed with the square notation. Graduale Simplex (Typis Polyglottis Vaticanus 1975) is suited to less ambitious choirs. It contains music for the various parts of the Mass in the form of simple antiphons and psalm verses.

Liber Hymnarius (Solesmes. 1974)

The hymns and invitatories of the Divine office, as used in monasteries. Where most books print the first verse of hymns with music and then simply give the text of the other verses, the hymnarius prints the music with each verse.

Antiphonale Monasticum (Solesmes. 1934)

Contains the texts and music for the Monastic Divine Office for the liturgical year. The Psalterium Monasticum contains the texts and antiphons of the office for ordinary time but according to the New Vulgate version of the psalms.

Kyriale (Solesmes. 1997)

The chants for the *Asperges, Vidi Aquam,* the *Kyrie, Gloria, Sanctus, Agnus Dei* of Masses I - XVIII, *Credo* I - VI, and other *ad libitum* chants.

Cantus Selecti (Solesmes)

A selection of the most accessible pieces from the Gregorian repertory for various occasions and the principal feasts of the year.

The Gregorian Missal for Sundays (Solesmes. 1990)

Containing all that is necessary for Sunday Mass and the major feasts. The full texts of the readings are not included though the scriptural references are given. The Kyriale is included, as are the Mass chants for each week with a vernacular translation beneath.

Liber Cantualis (Solesmes. 1983)

Brings together, in a small volume, the music of the Latin responses at Mass, a number of masses selected from the Kyriale, the chants of the requiem mass, the sequences, and other popular antiphons, hymns and chants.

Liber Cantualis comitante organo (Solesmes. 1983)

The chants of the Liber Cantualis with organ accompaniment.

Graduale Romanum comitante organo (Solesmes. 1984)

A three volume book of keyboard accompaniments to the Mass chants through the year by Abbé Ferdinand Portier. These provide useful, austere accompaniments which not only provide a foundation for good accompaniment skills but also are useful in that they contain the melody of the chant in modern notation.

Chant Theory

For those wishing to study the chant to a serious academic level, the following books will serve as useful starting points.

Gregorian Chant. Willi Apel. (Indiana 1990)

First published in 1958, this is now something of a classic work.

Western Plainchant, a handbook. David Hiley. (OUP 1993)

Widely accepted as the current standard textbook on the chant, Hiley adds to his impressive text a very useful and extensive bibliography.

Websites

www.osb.org is a useful website for those who wish either to follow its links concerning the chant, or seek out a monastery near to them in order to hear the chant live.

www.solesmes.com contains a short history of the chant, a real audio presentation of various chants, and an introduction to the enormous contribution of that abbey to the revival and study of Gregorian Chant in modern times.

www.stceciliasabbey.org.uk This English monastery of Benedictine nuns of the Congregation of Solesmes is noted for its excellence in the daily performance of the chant in the Mass and Office. Their website includes a regularly updated chant feature, with a recorded piece of chant and an explanation of its history and role in the liturgy.

Compact discs

A wide a range of recordings of varying quality is available. Those produced by the Abbeys of Solesmes and Fontgombault are reliable and to be commended to the reader. Two are particularly recommended here. The first as a general introduction, and the second for the quality of performance.

Learning about Gregorian Chant   **CD S 843**
Narration by Sarah Moule

Written by Dom Daniel Saulnier of the Abbey of Solesmes, and narrated by Sarah Moule, this CD guides the beginner through the basics concerning the chant, its history, musical forms and genres, and includes a generous selection of chant drawn from the vast collection of Solesmes recordings.

Solennité de Sainte Marie, Mère de Dieu   **AMCD 107/39701**
Monks of Fontgombault

An excellent introduction to the chant, this CD contains the chants of vespers for the January 1st feast of Mary, the Mother of God, along with Benediction chants and other antiphons, hymns and responsories. The accompanying booklet contains the text, French translation, and brief liturgical description, along with the music of the selected chants. The quality of the performance and of the recording is excellent, as is the subtle organ accompaniment to the psalmody. This is to be recommended to both the seasoned chant enthusiast and the beginner.